KT-415-241

Hitchcock Blonde

Terry Johnson

Methuen Drama

Published by Methuen 2003

1 3 5 7 9 10 8 6 4 2

First published in 2003 by
Methuen Publishing Limited,
215 Vauxhall Bridge Road,
London SW1V 1EJ

Copyright © Terry Johnson 2003

Terry Johnson has asserted his right under the Copyright, Designs
and Patents Act, 1988, to be identified as the author of this work

Methuen Publishing Limited Reg. No. 3543167

A CIP catalogue record is available from the British Library

ISBN 0 413 77356 6

Typeset by SX Composing DTP, Rayleigh, Essex
Printed and bound in Great Britain by
Cox & Wyman Ltd, Reading, Berkshire

Caution
All rights in this play are strictly reserved.
Application for performance, etc., should be made before rehearsals
begin to The Agency, 24 Pottery Lane, London W11 4LZ.
No performance may be given unless a licence has been obtained.

This book is sold subject to the condition that it shall not, by way of
trade or otherwise, be lent, resold, hired out, or otherwise circulated in
any form of binding or cover other than that in which it is published and
without a similar condition, including this condition, being imposed on
the subsequent purchaser.

ROYAL COURT

Royal Court Theatre presents

HITCHCOCK BLONDE

by **Terry Johnson**

First performance at the Royal Court Jerwood Theatre Downstairs
Sloane Square, London on 27 March 2003.

Supported by the Francis Finlay Foundation.

In association with Maidstone Productions and Sonia Friedman Productions.

The Royal Court would like to thank the following for their help with this production:
Beatwax, Moet & Chandon, Superdrug Stores plc, Lily Mollgaard, Greenwich Theatre, London Graphic Centre.

HITCHCOCK BLONDE

by **Terry Johnson**

Cast in order of appearance

1999	Nicola **Fiona Glascott**	
	Alex **David Haig**	
1959	Hitch **William Hootkins**	
	Blonde **Rosamund Pike**	
	Husband **Owen McDonnell**	
1919	Blonde **Victoria Gay**	
	Hitchcock **Alexander Delamere**	

Director **Terry Johnson**
Designer and Video Designer **William Dudley**
Lighting Designer **Simon Corder**
Sound Designer **Ian Dickinson**
Video Realisation **Dick Straker, Sven Ortel for Mesmer**
Video Post Production and Animation **Richard Kenyon**
Assistant Director **Katie Read**
Casting Director **Lisa Makin**
Production Manager **Paul Handley**
Stage Manager **Cal Hawes**
Deputy Stage Manager **Caroline Healey**
Assistant Stage Manager **Sharon Cooper**
Costume Supervisor **Iona Kenrick**
Fight Director **Terry King**
Dialect Coach **Jill McCullough**
Company Voice Work **Patsy Rodenburg**
Set built by **Weld - Fab Stage Engineering Ltd**
Set painted by **Richard Nutbourne**
Projection Equipment supplied by **XL Video**

1919

Director of Photography **David J.L.Odd**
Camera Operator **Tony Slater-Ling**
Stills Photographer **Gautier Deblonde**
Hair **Chrissi Turner**
Make-up **Chiara Guizzetti**
Props **Hannah Bentley, Nicole Keighley**
Gaffer **Johanna Town**
Catering **Diane Borger**
Runner **Natalie Abrahami**
Clapper/Runner **Alice Bailey Johnson**

THE COMPANY

Terry Johnson (writer and director)
For the Royal Court, as writer: Hysteria, Cries from the Mammal House, Insignificance.
Other plays include, as writer: Cleo, Camping, Emmanuelle and Dick, The London Cuckolds (RNT); Dead Funny (Hampstead/Vaudeville/West End tour); Imagine Drowning (Hampstead); Tuesday's Child (Theatre Royal, Stratford); Unsuitable for Adults; Amabel (Bush); Days Here So Dark (Paines Plough).
As director: The Graduate (Plymouth Theater /Broadway/Gielgud); Entertaining Mr Sloane (Arts); Sparkleshark (RNT); The Memory of Water (Hampstead/Vaudeville); Elton John's Glasses (Palace Theatre, Watford/Queen's); Cracked, The Memory of Water (Hampstead); The Libertine (Steppenwolf, Chicago); Just Between Ourselves, Ragdoll (Bristol Old Vic); Death of a Salesman (Theatre Royal, York).
Television includes: Cor Blimey!, The Bite, The Lorelei, Way Upstream.

Simon Corder (lighting designer)
Theatre includes: To Kill a Mockingbird (Theatr Clwyd); Entertaining Mr Sloane (Theatre Royal, Bath/West End); Les Enfants du Paradis (RSC); Cleo, Camping, Emmanuelle and Dick, London Cuckolds, Ends of the Earth (RNT); A Streetcar Named Desire (West End); The Robbers (Gate); The Letter (Lyric); After Darwin (Hampstead).
Opera includes: Cunning Little Vixen (ETO); Rodelinda (Opera Touring Company/Brooklyn Academy of Arts, USA); Don Giovanni (Holland Park Opera); A Village Romeo and Juliet (Cagliari, Sardinia); La Traviata (Mid Wales Opera); The Snow Queen, Postcards from Morocco (Guildhall); Mephistopheles (ENO/Buenos Aires); Aida (Earl's Court/Seville/Lisbon/Helsinki/Buenos Aires); The Vanishing Bridegroom (Scottish Opera); The Blackened Man (Linbury).
Dance includes: 3 (Cholmondeleys); The Featherstonehaughs Draw on the Sketchbooks of Egon Schiele (The Featherstonehaughs).

Alexander Delamere
Theatre includes: The Rise and Fall of Little Voice (Oldham Coliseum); Oliver, A Christmas Carol (Liverpool Playhouse); Lautrec (Shaftesbury); Perfect Pitch, Anna Karenina (Bolton Octagon); West Side Story (Plymouth/West End); Pinocchio, Hard Times, Elsie and Norm's Macbeth, Peter Pan (Swan, Worcester); An Evening with Gary Lineker (Derby Playhouse/Everyman, Cheltenham); Macbeth, The Red Balloon, Pygmalion (Birmingham Rep); The Wonderland Adventures of Alice (London Bubble); A Family Affair (Theatr Clwyd); A Christmas Carol (Library, Manchester); Fiddler on the Roof (Belgrade, Coventry); Pal Joey (Theatre Royal, York).
Television includes: Emmerdale, Coronation Street, Holby City, The Bill, The Clothes Show.
Film includes: 28 Days Later.
Radio includes: The Day I Finished Off Charlotte Bronte, Letters to an Icon, The History Man.

Ian Dickinson (sound designer)
For the Royal Court: Terrorism, Black Milk, Crazyblackmuthafuckin'self, Caryl Churchill Season, Imprint, Mother Teresa is Dead, Push Up, Workers Writes, Fucking Games, Herons, Cutting Through the Carnival.
Other theatre includes: Port (Royal Exchange Manchester); Night of the Soul (RSC Barbican); Eyes of the Kappa (Gate); Crime and Punishment in Dalston (Arcola Theatre); Search and Destroy (New End, Hampstead); Phaedra, Three Sisters, The Shaughraun, Writer's Cramp (Royal Lyceum, Edinburgh); The Whore's Dream (RSC Fringe, Edinburgh); As You Like It, An Experienced Woman Gives Advice, Present Laughter, The Philadelphia Story, Wolks World, Poor Superman, Martin Yesterday, Fast Food, Coyote Ugly, Prizenight (Royal Exchange, Manchester); Great Monsters of Western Street (Throat Theatre Company); Small Craft Warnings, Tieble and Her Demon (Manchester Evening News Theatre Awards Best Design Team), The Merchant of Venice, Death and The Maiden (Library Theatre Company, Manchester).
Ian is Head of Sound at the Royal Court.

William Dudley (designer and video designer)

For the Royal Court: The York Realist (English Touring Theatre), Small Change, The Fool, Edmund, Hamlet, Etta Jenks, Kafka's Dick, I Licked A Slag's Deodorant (Ambassadors). Other theatre includes: Ivanov, That Good Between Us, Richard III, The Party, The Merry Wives of Windsor, Richard II, A Midsummer Night's Dream, Country Dancing, The General from America, Marya (Old Vic), Hamlet (Neue Schauspielhaus Hamburg), The Ship, The Big Picnic (RSC); The Breath of Life, Blue/Orange, Entertaining Mr Sloane, Lenny, A Streetcar Named Desire, Rat in the Skull, My Night With Reg, Amdeus, Heartbreak House, Matador, Girlfriends, Kiss Me Kate, Mutiny!, I Claudius (West End); The Coast of Utopia, All My Sons, The Forest, Cleo, Camping, Emmanuelle and Dick, The London Cuckolds, The Homecoming, The Alchemist, Mary Stuart, Wild Oats, Under Milk Wood, Johnny on a Spot, On the Ledge, The Rise and Fall of Little Voice, Pygmalion, The Coup, The Crucible, The Voysey Inheritance, Bartholomew Fair, The Changeling, The Shaughran, Cat on a Hot Tin Roof, Waiting for Godot, Entertaining Strangers, The Mysteries, The Critic, The Real Inspector Hound, Schweyk in the Second World War, Don Quixote, Dispatches, Undiscovered Country, The World Turned Upside Down, Lost Worlds, Larkrise to Candleford, Lavender Blue (RNT); Some Sunny Day (Hampstead); The Deep Blue Sea, Tongue of A Bird (Almeida).
Film includes: Persuasion, The Rose Theatre.
Opera includes: Idomeneo (WNO), Billy Budd (Metropolitan Opera), Barber of Seville, Seraglio (Glyndebourne), Tales of Hoffman, Der Rosenkavalier, Don Giovanni, The Cunning Little Vixen (ROH), The Ring Cycle (Bayreuth), Un Ballo in Masquera (Salzburg Festival), Lucia di Lammermoor (Lyric Opera of Chicago/Opera National de Paris), The Silver Tassie (ENO).

Victoria Gay

Theatre includes: The Nerd (Objective); Fool to Yourself (Scarborough); A Midsummer Night's Dream, Noises Off, Billy Liar, Dracula, Wind in the Willows (Liverpool Playhouse); Charley's Aunt, Chorus of Disapproval, Wuthering Heights, First Class Passenger (Pitlochry); Under Milkwood (Wimbledon).
Television includes: Silent Witness, Where the Heart Is, Numbertime, Prince & Pauper, Revelations.
Film includes: Plunge, The Real Thing.

Fiona Glascott

Theatre includes: Mahler's Conversion (Aldwych); A Life (Abbey, Dublin/National Tour); The Shaughraun (Royal Lyceum, Edinburgh); The Spirit of Annie Ross (Gate, Dublin); The Seagull (The Corn Exchange, Dublin); Bananas in the Breadbin (Barnstorm, Kilkenny); Henry V, A Midsummer Night's Dream, The Sea (Dublin).
Television includes: Batchelors Wharf, The Bill, Any Time Now, Fair City, Making the Cut, Ballykissangel, Flesh and Blood.
Film includes: Chasing the Dragon, Goldfish Memory, Judas and Jesus, Resident Evil, Fatboy & Twintub, (Special commendation Cork Film Festival 2000), Magnificent Ambersons, Forecourt, Meteor, This is My Father, Crushproof.
Radio includes: The Bacchae, Cybermom, The Playboy of the Western World, Malachy's Money.

David Haig

For the Royal Court: Our Country's Good (Olivier Award), The Recruiting Officer, Greenland, Tom and Viv (Broadway).
Other theatre includes: Life x 3(Tour/West End); House and Garden, Fair Ladies at a Game of Poem Cards, Berenice (RNT); Art (West End /Broadway); My Boy Jack (Hampstead); Dead Funny (Hampstead/West End); Measure for Measure, A Midsummer Night's Dream, World's Apart, Every Man in His Humour, Time of Your Life, Volpone (RSC).
Television includes: Crime and Punishment, Station Jim, Talking Heads - Playing Sandwiches, The Thin Blue Line, Portrait of a Marriage, Soldier, Soldier, Love on a Branch Line, Keeping Mum, Cracker, Inspector Morse, Wycliffe, Inspector Alleyn Mystery, A Flame to the Phoenix, Badger, Campion, Diamonds, Chessgame, Darling Buds of May.
Film includes: Two Weeks Notice, Four Weddings and a Funeral, Lady Jane, Morons from Outer Space.

William Hootkins

For the Royal Court: Insignificance, The Dentist, The Watergate Tapes.

Other theatre includes: Orpheus Descending (Donmar); Our Betters (Chichester); Hotel Arusha (Nuffield); Their Finest Hour (English Chamber Theatre); What A Way to Run A Revolution (RSC/Cockpit); Domino Theory (ICA); Dreams in an Empty City (Lyric); The Homecoming, A Man for All Seasons, Moby Dick, A Flea in Her Ear, (Summer Intime, NJ); Deathtrap (Dallas Theater Genter); A Funny Thing Happened on the Way to the Forum (Santa Fe, New Mexico).

Television includes: Like Father, Like Santa, Cheers, The Young Indiana Jones, Poirot, Cagney & Lacey, Taxi, Chancer, The Big Knife, The New Statesman, The Life & Times of David Lloyd George, Blackadder, Black Carrion, Paradise Postponed, Rocket to the Moon, Come Back Little Sheba, Capital City, Rabbit Pie Day, The Ambassadors, Bergerac, The Paradise Run, Waco & Rhinhart, Marlowe: Private Eye, The Tempest, Bret Maverick, Remington Steele, Monkeys, Partners in Crime, Tales of the Unexpected, The Lost Boys, Clouds of Glory, Before Water Lilies, Lillie, Oppenheimer, Speed King, The Return of Sherlock Holmes, Billion Dollar Bubble.

Film includes: Three Men in A Restaurant, The Magnificent Ambersons, Town & Country, The Omega Code, This World, Then the Fireworks, Island of Dr Moreau, Death Machine, Something to Believe In, Age of Treason, Dust Devil, A River Runs Through It, Hear My Song, Batman, Biggles, Water, Hardware, Crusoe, American Gothic, Dreamchild, White Nights, Trail of the Pink Panther, Curse of the Pink Panther, Raiders of the Lost Ark, Valentino, Superman, Bad Timing, Hanover Street, Flash Gordon, Zina, Roosevelt, The Lady Vanishes, Twilight's Last Gleaming, Hussy, Star Wars.

Owen McDonnell

Theatre includes: Les Liaisons Dangereuses (Liverpool Playhouse); This Property is Condemned (Bewley's Cafe Theatre, Dublin); Big Maggie (Abbey, Dublin); Barbaric Comedies (Abbey, Dublin/Edinburgh International Festival); Antigone (Old Vic); Death of A Salesman (Birmingham Rep); The Chair (Cochrane).
Film includes: Conspiracy of Silence.

Rosamund Pike

Television includes: Foyle's War, Love in a Cold Climate, A Rather English Marriage, Trial and Retribution IV, Wives and Daughters.
Film includes: Die Another Day.

Katie Read (assistant director)

As assistant director, theatre includes: The Coast of Utopia, The Walls (RNT).
As director, theatre includes: The Country Doctor (RNT); Pains of Youth (RNT Studio); Blue Remembered Hills, The Libertine (BAC).

THE ENGLISH STAGE COMPANY
AT THE ROYAL COURT

The English Stage Company at the Royal Court opened in 1956 as a subsidised theatre producing new British plays, international plays and some classical revivals.

The first artistic director George Devine aimed to create a writers' theatre, 'a place where the dramatist is acknowledged as the fundamental creative force in the theatre and where the play is more important than the actors, the director, the designer'. The urgent need was to find a contemporary style in which the play, the acting, direction and design are all combined. He believed that 'the battle will be a long one to continue to create the right conditions for writers to work in'.

Devine aimed to discover 'hard-hitting, uncompromising writers whose plays are stimulating, provocative and exciting'. The Royal Court production of John Osborne's Look Back in Anger in May 1956 is now seen as the decisive starting point of modern British drama and the policy created a new generation of British playwrights. The first wave included John Osborne, Arnold Wesker, John Arden, Ann Jellicoe, N F Simpson and Edward Bond. Early seasons included new international plays by Bertolt Brecht, Eugène Ionesco, Samuel Beckett, Jean-Paul Sartre and Marguerite Duras.

The theatre started with the 400-seat proscenium arch Theatre Downstairs, and then in 1969 opened a second theatre, the 60-seat studio Theatre Upstairs. Some productions transfer to the West End, such as Caryl Churchill's Far Away, Conor McPherson's The Weir, Kevin Elyot's Mouth to Mouth and My Night With Reg. The Royal Court also co-produces plays which have transferred to the West End or toured internationally, such as Sebastian Barry's The Steward of Christendom and Mark Ravenhill's Shopping and Fucking (with Out of Joint), Martin McDonagh's The Beauty Queen Of Leenane (with Druid Theatre Company), Ayub Khan-Din's East is East (with Tamasha Theatre Company, and now a feature film).

Since 1994 the Royal Court's artistic policy has again been vigorously directed to finding and producing a new generation of playwrights. The writers include Joe Penhall, Rebecca Prichard, Michael Wynne, Nick Grosso, Judy Upton, Meredith Oakes, Sarah Kane, Anthony Neilson, Judith Johnson, James Stock, Jez Butterworth, Marina Carr, Phyllis Nagy, Simon Block, Martin McDonagh, Mark Ravenhill, Ayub Khan-Din, Tamantha Hammerschlag, Jess Walters, Che Walker, Conor McPherson, Simon Stephens,

photo: Andy Chopping

Richard Bean, Roy Williams, Gary Mitchell, Mick Mahoney, Rebecca Gilman, Christopher Shinn, Kia Corthron, David Gieselmann, Marius von Mayenburg, David Eldridge, Leo Butler, Zinnie Harris, Grae Cleugh, Roland Schimmelpfennig, Vassily Sigarev and The Presynakov Brothers. This expanded programme of new plays has been made possible through the support of A.S.K Theater Projects, the Jerwood Charitable Foundation, the American Friends of the Royal Court Theatre and many in association with the Royal National Theatre Studio.

In recent years there have been record-breaking productions at the box office, with capacity houses for Caryl Churchill's A Number, Jez Butterworth's The Night Heron, Rebecca Gilman's Boy Gets Girl, Kevin Elyot's Mouth To Mouth, David Hare's My Zinc Bed and Conor McPherson's The Weir, which transferred to the West End in October 1998 and ran for nearly two years at the Duke of York's Theatre.

The newly refurbished theatre in Sloane Square opened in February 2000, with a policy still inspired by the first artistic director George Devine. The Royal Court is an international theatre for new plays and new playwrights, and the work shapes contemporary drama in Britain and overseas.

AWARDS FOR
THE ROYAL COURT

Jez Butterworth won the 1995 George Devine Award, the Writers' Guild New Writer of the Year Award, the Evening Standard Award for Most Promising Playwright and the Olivier Award for Best Comedy for Mojo.

The Royal Court was the overall winner of the 1995 Prudential Award for the Arts for creativity, excellence, innovation and accessibility. The Royal Court Theatre Upstairs won the 1995 Peter Brook Empty Space Award for innovation and excellence in theatre.

Michael Wynne won the 1996 Meyer-Whitworth Award for The Knocky. Martin McDonagh won the 1996 George Devine Award, the 1996 Writers' Guild Best Fringe Play Award, the 1996 Critics' Circle Award and the 1996 Evening Standard Award for Most Promising Playwright for The Beauty Queen of Leenane. Marina Carr won the 19th Susan Smith Blackburn Prize (1996/7) for Portia Coughlan. Conor McPherson won the 1997 George Devine Award, the 1997 Critics' Circle Award and the 1997 Evening Standard Award for Most Promising Playwright for The Weir. Ayub Khan-Din won the 1997 Writers' Guild Awards for Best West End Play and Writers' Guild New Writer of the Year and the 1996 John Whiting Award for East is East (co-production with Tamasha).

At the 1998 Tony Awards, Martin McDonagh's The Beauty Queen of Leenane (co-production with Druid Theatre Company) won four awards including Garry Hynes for Best Director and was nominated for a further two. Eugene Ionesco's The Chairs (co-production with Theatre de Complicite) was nominated for six Tony awards. David Hare won the 1998 Time Out Live Award for Outstanding Achievement and six awards in New York including the Drama League, Drama Desk and New York Critics Circle Award for Via Dolorosa. Sarah Kane won the 1998 Arts Foundation Fellowship in Playwriting. Rebecca Prichard won the 1998 Critics' Circle Award for Most Promising Playwright for Yard Gal (co-production with Clean Break).
Conor McPherson won the 1999 Olivier Award for Best New Play for The Weir. The Royal Court won the 1999 ITI Award for Excellence in International Theatre. Sarah Kane's Cleansed was judged Best Foreign Language Play in 1999 by Theater Heute in Germany. Gary Mitchell won the 1999 Pearson Best Play Award for Trust. Rebecca Gilman was joint winner of the 1999 George Devine Award and won the 1999 Evening Standard Award for Most Promising Playwright for The Glory of Living.

In 1999, the Royal Court won the European theatre prize New Theatrical Realities, presented at Taormina Arte in Sicily, for its efforts in recent years in discovering and producing the work of young British dramatists.

Roy Williams and Gary Mitchell were joint winners of the George Devine Award 2000 for Most Promising Playwright for Lift Off and The Force of Change respectively. At the Barclays Theatre Awards 2000 presented by the TMA, Richard Wilson won the Best Director Award for David Gieselmann's Mr Kolpert and Jeremy Herbert won the Best Designer Award for Sarah Kane's 4.48 Psychosis. Gary Mitchell won the Evening Standard's Charles Wintour Award 2000 for Most Promising Playwright for The Force of Change. Stephen Jeffreys' I Just Stopped by to See The Man won an AT&T: On Stage Award 2000.

David Eldridge's Under the Blue Sky won the Time Out Live Award 2001 for Best New Play in the West End. Leo Butler won the George Devine Award 2001 for Most Promising Playwright for Redundant. Roy Williams won the Evening Standard's Charles Wintour Award 2001 for Most Promising Playwright for Clubland. Grae Cleugh won the 2001 Olivier Award for Most Promising Playwright for Fucking Games. Richard Bean was joint winner of the George Devine Award 2002 for Most Promising Playwright for Under the Whaleback. Caryl Churchill won the 2002 Evening Standard Award for Best New Play for A Number. Vassily Sigarev won the 2002 Evening Standard Charles Wintour Award for Most Promising Playwright for Plasticine. Ian MacNeil won the 2002 Evening Standard Award for Best Design for A Number and Plasticine. Peter Gill won the 2002 Critics' Circle Award for Best New Play for The York Realist (English Touring Theatre).

ROYAL COURT BOOKSHOP

The bookshop offers a wide range of playtexts and theatre books, with over 1,000 titles. Located in the downstairs Bar and Food area, the bookshop is open Monday to Saturday, afternoons and evenings.

Many Royal Court playtexts are available for just £2 including works by Harold Pinter, Caryl Churchill, Rebecca Gilman, Martin Crimp, Sarah Kane, Conor McPherson, Ayub Khan-Din, Timberlake Wertenbaker and Roy Williams.

For information on titles and special events, Email: bookshop@royalcourttheatre.com
Tel: 020 7565 5024

THE AMERICAN FRIENDS OF THE ROYAL COURT THEATRE

AFRCT support the mission of the Royal Court and are primarily focused on raising funds to enable the theatre to produce new work by emerging American writers. Since this not-for-profit organisation was founded in 1997, AFRCT has contributed to nine productions. They have also supported the participation of young artists in the Royal Court's acclaimed International Residency.

If you would like to support the ongoing work of the Royal Court, please contact the Development Department on 020 7565 5050.

AMERICAN FRIENDS
Founders
Harry Brown and Richard Walsh
Francis Finlay
Amanda Foreman and Jonathan Barton
Monica Gerard-Sharp and Ali Wambold
Jeananne Hauswald
Mary Ellen Johnson and Richard Goeltz
Dany Khosrovani
William and Kay Koplovitz
Laura Pels
Ben Rauch and Margaret Scott
Mr. and Mrs. Gerald Schoenfeld

Patrons
Arthur Bellinzoni
Linda Bialecki and Douglas Klassen
Catherine Curran
Mr. and Mrs. Robert Donnalley
William and Ursula Fairbairn
Mr. and Mrs. Richard Grand
Sahra Lese
Susan Marks
Mr. and Mrs. Hamish Maxwell
Jeff and Cynthia Penney
Sylvia Scheuer
Amy Weinstein
Katheryn Williams

Benefactors
Rachael Bail
Mr. and Mrs. Matthew Chapman
David Day and John Drummond
T. Richard Fishbein and Estelle Bender
Jennifer Laing

Imelda Liddiard
Rhonda and Robert Sherman
Mika Sterling
Chuck Wentzel and Kevin Fullerton

Members
Jon Armstrong
Eleanor Cicerchi
Christopher Flacke
Nancy Flinn
Rochelle Ohrstrom
Mr. and Mrs. Daniel Okrent
Tim Runion and Vipul Nishawala
David and Patricia Smalley

American Friends Development Director
Timothy Runion
Tel: +1 212 408 0465

ROYAL COURT
JERWOOD THEATRE DOWNSTAIRS

12 June - 12 July 2003
FALLOUT
by Roy Williams

A boy is found dead. D.C. Joe Stephens must return to his old neighbourhood to investigate. Shanice is avoiding his questions about her boyfriend, Emile, and his mates. Ronnie saw something, but promised Shanice she'd say nothing. But when a reward is offered, keeping quiet is a major test of their street loyalty.

A new play from award-winning playwright Roy Williams.

JERWOOD THEATRE UPSTAIRS

10 April - 3 May 2003
UNDER THE WHALEBACK
by Richard Bean

15 May - 7 June 2003
FLESH WOUND
by Che Walker

19 June - 12 July 2003
FOOD CHAIN
by Mick Mahoney

Box Office 020 7565 5000
www.royalcourttheatre.com

London Government

ARTS COUNCIL ENGLAND

PROGRAMME SUPPORTERS

The Royal Court (English Stage Company Ltd) receives its principal funding from London Arts. It is also supported financially by a wide range of private companies and public bodies and earns the remainder of its income from the box office and its own trading activities.

The Royal Borough of Kensington & Chelsea gives an annual grant to the Royal Court Young Writers' Programme and the Affiliation of London Government provides project funding for a number of play development initiatives.

The Jerwood Charitable Foundation continues to support new plays by new playwrights through the Jerwood New Playwrights series. Since 1993 the A.S.K. Theater Projects of Los Angeles has funded a Playwrights' Programme at the theatre. Bloomberg Mondays, the Royal Court's reduced price ticket scheme, is supported by Bloomberg. Over the past seven years the BBC has supported the Gerald Chapman Fund for directors.

ROYAL COURT
DEVELOPMENT BOARD
Tamara Ingram (Chair)
Jonathan Cameron
(Vice Chair)
Timothy Burrill
Anthony Burton
Jonathan Caplan QC
Deborah Davis
Cecily Engle
Joseph Fiennes
Kimberly Fortier
Joyce Hytner
Dan Klein
Michael Potter
Ben Rauch
Mark Robinson
William Russell
Sue Stapely
James L Tanner
Will Turner

TRUSTS AND FOUNDATIONS
American Friends of the Royal
Court Theatre
A.S.K Theater Projects
The Carnegie United
Kingdom Trust
Carlton Television Trust
Gerald Chapman Fund
The Foundation for Sport and
the Arts
Genesis Foundation
The Goldsmiths' Company
The Haberdashers' Company
Paul Hamlyn Foundation
Jerwood Charitable
Foundation
John Lyon's Charity
The Mercers' Company
The Laura Pels Foundation
Quercus Charitable Trust
The Peggy Ramsay
Foundation
The Eva & Hans K Rausing
Trust
The Royal Victoria Hall
Foundation
The Peter Jay Sharp
Foundation
The Sobell Foundation
The Trusthouse Charitable
Foundation
Garfield Weston Foundation
Worshipful Company of
Information Technologists

MAJOR SPONSORS
American Airlines
Barclays
BBC
Bloomberg
Channel Four
Lever Fabergé
Royal College of Psychiatrists

BUSINESS MEMBERS
Aviva plc
BP
Lazard
McCann-Erickson
Pemberton Greenish
Peter Jones
Redwood
Siemens
Simons Muirhead & Burton
Slaughter and May

MEDIA MEMBERS
Beatwax
Columbia Tristar Films (UK)
Hat Trick Productions

PRODUCTION SYNDICATE
Anonymous
Jonathan & Sindy Caplan
Kay Hartenstein Saatchi
Richard & Susan Hayden
Kadee Robbins
William & Hilary Russell

INDIVIDUAL MEMBERS
Patrons
Anonymous
Advanpress
Ms Kay Ellen Consolver
Coppard and Co.
Mrs Philip Donald
Tom & Simone Fenton
Homevale Ltd
Mr & Mrs Jack Keenan
Richard & Robin Landsberger
New Penny Productions Ltd
Caroline Quentin
Ian & Carol Sellars
Jan & Michael Topham

Benefactors
Martha Allfrey
Anonymous
Jeremy & Amanda Attard-
Manché
Matilde Attolico

Jasper Boersma
Brian Boylan
Katie Bradford
Julian Brookstone
Lucy Bryn Davies
Danielle Byrne
Yven-Wei Chew
Martin Cliff
Peter Czernin
Robyn Durie
Winston & Jean Fletcher
Joachim Fleury
Charlotte & Nick Fraser
Judy & Frank Grace
Amanda Howard Associates
Ltd.
Tamara Ingram
Peter & Maria Kellner
Ann Lewis
Barbara Minto
Paul Oppenheimer
Janet & Michael Orr
Maria Peacock
Jeremy Priestley
Simon Rebbechi
Kate Richardson
Nigel Seale
Jenny Sheridan
Peregrine Simon
Brian D Smith
Amanda Vail
Thai Ping Wong
George & Moira Yip
Georgia Zaris

Associates
Anonymous
Eleanor Bowen
Mrs Elly Brook JP
Ossi & Paul Burger
Mrs Helena Butler
Carole & Neville Conrad
Margaret Cowper
Barry Cox
Andrew Cryer
Mr & Mrs Daitz
David Day
Zoë Dominic
Jacqueline & Jonathan
Gestetner
Michael Goddard
Vivien Goodwin

Sue & Don Guiney
Phil Hobbs - LTRC
Tarek J. Kassem
Carole A. Leng
Lady Lever
Colette & Peter Levy
Mr Watcyn Lewis
Christopher Marcus
David Marks
Nicola McFarland
Mr & Mrs Roderick A
McManigal
Eva Monley
Pat Morton
Gavin & Ann Neath
Georgia Oetker
Lyndy Payne
Pauline Pinder
William Poeton CBE &
Barbara Poeton
Michael Potter
John Ritchie
Bernard Shapero
Kathleen Shiach
Lois Sieff OBE
Sue Stapely
Peter & Prilla Stott
Carl & Martha Tack
Will Turner
Anthony Wigram

STAGE HANDS CIRCLE
Graham Billing
Andrew Cryer
Lindy Fletcher
Susan & Richard
Hayden
Mr R Hopkins
Philip Hughes Trust
Dr A V Jones
Roger Jospe
Miss A Lind-Smith
Mr J Mills
Nevin Charitable Trust
Janet & Michael Orr
Jeremy Priestley
Ann Scurfield
Brian Smith
Harry Streets
Thai Ping Wong
Richard Wilson OBE
C C Wright

FOR THE ROYAL COURT

Royal Court Theatre, Sloane Square, London SW1W 8AS
Tel: 020 7565 5050 Fax: 020 7565 5001
info@royalcourttheatre.com
www.royalcourttheatre.com

ARTISTIC
Artistic Director **Ian Rickson**
Associate Director International **Elyse Dodgson**
Associate Director Casting **Lisa Makin**
Associate Directors* **Stephen Daldry, James Macdonald, Katie Mitchell, Max Stafford-Clark, Richard Wilson**
Literary Manager **Graham Whybrow**
Resident Dramatist **Michael Wynne**
Trainee Associate Directors **Femi Elufowoju, Jnr., Josie Rourke§**
Voice Associate **Patsy Rodenburg***
Casting Assistant **Amy Ball**
International Administrator **Ushi Bagga**
International Associate **Ramin Gray**

YOUNG WRITERS' PROGRAMME
Associate Director **Ola Animashawun**
Administrator **Nina Lyndon**
Outreach Worker **Lucy Dunkerley**
Education Officer **Emily McLaughlin**
Writers Tutor **Simon Stephens***

PRODUCTION
Production Manager **Paul Handley**
Deputy Production Manager **Sue Bird**
Production Assistant **Hannah Bentley**
Facilities Manager **Fran McElroy**
Facilities Deputy **Adair Ballantine**
Head of Lighting **Johanna Town**
Lighting Deputy **Trevor Wallace**
Assistant Electricians **Gavin Owen, Andrew Taylor**
Lighting Board Operator **Sam Shortt**
Head of Stage **Martin Riley**
Stage Deputy **Steven Stickler**
Stage Chargehand **Daniel Lockett**
Head of Sound **Ian Dickinson**
Sound Deputy **Emma Laxton**
Head of Wardrobe **Iona Kenrick**
Wardrobe Deputy **Jackie Orton**

MANAGEMENT
Executive Director **Barbara Matthews**
Executive Assistant **Nia Janis**
General Manager **Diane Borger**
Finance Director **Sarah Preece**
Finance Officer **Rachel Harrison**
Finance Assistant **Martin Wheeler**
Accountant **Simone De Bruyker***
Administrative Assistant **Natalie Abrahami**

MARKETING & PRESS
Head of Marketing **Penny Mills**
Head of Press **Ewan Thomson**
Marketing and Press Officer **Charlotte Franklin**
Marketing Assistant **Alix Hearn**
Box Office Manager **Neil Grutchfield**
Deputy Box Office Manager **Valli Dakshinamurthi**
Duty Box Office Manager **Glen Bowman**
Box Office Sales Operators **Carol Pritchard, Steven Kuleshnyk**
Press and Marketing Intern **Day Macaskill**

DEVELOPMENT
Head of Development **Helen Salmon**
Development Associate **Susan Davenport***
Sponsorship Manager **Rebecca Preston***
Sponsorship Associate (Maternity cover) **Jeremy Goldstein***
Sponsorship Officer **Chris James**
Development Officer **Alex Lawson**
Events Assistant **Eleanor Lloyd**

FRONT OF HOUSE
Theatre Manager **Elizabeth Brown**
Deputy Theatre Manager **Daniel McHale**
Duty House Managers* **Paul McLaughlin, Alan Gilmour**
Bookshop Manager **Simon David**
Assistant Bookshop Manager **Edin Suljic***
Bookshop Assistants* **Michael Chance, Jennie Fellows**
Stage Door/Reception **Simon David, Kat Smiley, Tyrone Lucas, Jon Hunter**

Thanks to all of our box office assistants and ushers

* part-time
§ The Trainee Associate Director Bursaries are supported by the Quercus Trust.

ENGLISH STAGE COMPANY
President
Jocelyn Herbert

Vice President
Joan Plowright CBE

Honorary Council
Sir Richard Eyre
Alan Grieve
Sir John Mortimer CBE QC

Council
Chairwoman **Liz Calder**
Vice-Chairman **Anthony Burton**

Members
Judy Daish
Graham Devlin
Joyce Hytner
Tamara Ingram
Phyllida Lloyd
James Midgley
Sophie Okonedo
Edward Miliband
Katharine Viner
Nicholas Wright

Hitchcock Blonde

Hitchcock Blonde premiered at The Royal Court Theatre
London on 2nd April, 2003. The cast was as follows:

1999	**Nicola**	Fiona Glascott
	Alex	David Haig
1959	**Hitch**	William Hootkins
	Blonde	Rosamund Pike
	Husband	Owen McDonnell
1919	**Blonde**	Victoria Gay
	Hitchcock	Alexander Delamere

Director   Terry Johnson
Designer and Video Designer   William Dudley
Lighting Designer   Simon Corder
Sound Designer   Ian Dickinson

Characters

Alex, *late forties*
Nicola, *early twenties*
Blonde, *late twenties*
Hitch, *late forties*
Husband, *late twenties*

Settings

1999
A small dark study
A large white villa

1959
Sound stage
Kitchen
Terrace
Inner sanctum

Music

Bernard Herrmann (or *homage*)

Act One

Scene One

1999. Iris out into small room in a wide black void. **Alex***'s study in a 1960s building.* **Nicola***, early twenties, reads an essay.* **Alex***, late forties, dressed late thirties, gazes out of a window to whiteness beyond.*

Nicola Opening shot, first angle: her torso, the knife, twenty-one frames. Second shot: tight close-up of mother, twenty-seven frames. Third shot: tighter version of first angle, the promise of her breasts, brackets, unfulfilled, brackets; twelve frames. Fourth shot, third angle, top shot, fourteen frames; time enough to register not the nipple but the knife that obscures it. Fifth shot: close-up of her face. Forty-nine frames. The Body Double cutaways involve nine set-ups. Close-up of her back, framed by shower curtain, arm and knife in foreground. Shallow focus top shot; her full torso; she struggles with mother. Medium close-up of both arms, one naked, one with knife, victim's body in background. Focus remains shallow; only the knife is sharp. Close-up of her belly; the knife slashes in and out of frame. Big close-up, two blades: her shoulder, the knife. Top shot of her legs and the blood. Blood hits the floor of the shower. Two tight handshots: one pressed against the tiling, the other grabs the shower curtain. Another top shot as she slides into the bath.

Alex Nicola.

Nicola Yes?

Alex You copied this out of a book.

Nicola I didn't.

Alex I wrote it.

Nicola Oh. Seminal.

Alex Thank you.

Nicola   You said to include a shot breakdown, so I did. Fundamentally anal, but hey; you're the expert. I spilt a Diet Coke. I lost my library privileges. I have to copy longhand, I get confused.

Alex   Anything original?

Nicola   'The contribution of the actual leading lady in the midst of all this carnage is dictated by a gentile modesty. This denotes less the presence of a gentleman than a presumed reticence on the part of the performer to get her tits out. Paradoxically, it's the body double who, by remaining anonymous, allows us the illusion of intimacy. We become intimate with our actual leading lady only at the moment of her death which, presuming she dies while we're looking into her eyes, is 888 frames later.'

Alex   So what's your hypothesis?

Nicola   Hitchcock and the Blonde.

Alex   What about them?

Nicola   He finally got one.

Alex   That's your conclusion?

Nicola   'Thirty-seven seconds. One of the pivotal cultural events of the twentieth century. An expression of misogyny so extreme, yet so precise, that with thirty-three stabs to the bone it pre-augurs four decades of butchery to come. For the very first time, the violent and vivid murder of a woman is depicted for the sheer thrill of it. In its thoughtful calculation it reveals a depth of hatred for its subject previously unparalleled. The moment remains hugely popular and has achieved mythic status due entirely, one must suspect, to the pleasure induced by watching it.'

She gives him the essay.

Not to mention the nightmares.

Alex   Pursued along dark corridors?

Nicola   Cornered. Intense confrontations. Tangled conversations. Huge feelings of guilt, no memories of why. Sort of dreams that take you so far down you barely surface until you've had a good cup of coffee.

Alex   I'll need your extended semiotics on my desk, before you disappear for the summer.

Nicola   Do my best.

Alex   Holiday?

Nicola   Home.

Alex   Bradford.

Nicola   Oldham. B *minus*?

She hands the essay back.

I can't do Ibiza. It's contagious.

Alex   What is?

Nicola   Bad behaviour. Half the year's off to Ibiza.

Alex   Ibiza.

He adds a pen-stroke and hands it back again.

Nicola   Didn't hurt, did it?

Alex   Is Ibiza as . . . ?

Nicola   If your idea of fun's having lager poured down your T-shirt.

Alex   I'd heard it was . . .

Nicola   It's crap. Unless you like vomit and wankers. Slags from Leeds slapping you in the toilet. Mindless shagging.

Alex   Well, the mindless shagging sounds all right.

Nicola   You can't have that on its own. It only comes with the vomit, slags and wankers. Why are we talking about shagging?

Alex   I've no idea.

Nicola   Bye then.

Alex   I've got a little villa.

Nicola   Have you?

Alex   Yes. It's on Kalithia.

Nicola   Lovely.

He shows her a photo.

Lovely.

Alex   Kalithia means beauty. Beautiful view.

Nicola   Looks fantastic.

Alex   It's unspoilt.

Nicola   Looks it. Lovely.

Alex   I have a proposition for you.

Nicola   What?

Alex   I'm on the acquisitions committee of the BFI, for whom I recently purchased a private archive. Alexander Lazaris was a Greek collector with an enthusiasm for memorabilic drivel, but I put in a bid because one of his major purchases in the early fifties was, ironically enough, the Gainsborough Library.

Nicola   As in Studios?

Alex   I suppose the Department of Culture might have prevented our cinematic heritage being sold off to a Greek shipping magnate had we in fact had a Department of Culture in 1952, but in any case the library was rumoured to be rubbish and Lazaris mad as a snake, so no one knows to this day what he actually picked up. I met him on Kalithia, in a bar. He was eighty and he'd been blind for almost twenty years. I went out on a limb with the acquisitions budget and secured, sight sadly unseen, the contents of his cellar.

Nicola   The Gainsborough Library?

Alex *produces a 16mm film canister, rusted with age. The tape that should seal the can, brittle and stained. The label, filthy, flyblown; hanging on by adhesive tape long since dried and useless. In spite of its decayed condition, the object has an aged, magical quality; it's an artefact.*

Alex   The rest of it's still on the island. Celluloid's unstable. Store it too cold it ossifies and splits. Let it get damp, it turns to slime. Dry it out, the print crumbles. Well, beneath the Villa Lazaris is evidently not so much a cellar as a modest canal. All the canisters are oxidised, half the seals are broken.

Nicola   And this is pre-war?

Alex   I'd guess around 1919.

Nicola   I'd guess you blew your acquisitions budget.

Alex   That's what I thought.

Nicola   Bought a pig in a poke and took home a pork pie.

Alex   I intend to spend the summer cataloguing.

Nicola   Poor you.

Alex   Might salvage a few good frames per thousand feet. Then I thought, why do it on my own? It's within your field of interest.

Nicola   I wrote an essay on restoration in the cafeteria. You gave it D minus. I wouldn't call it a major field of interest.

Alex   You romanticised a technical process. You were hostage to theory. Unenlightened by practice. Which is why you should come to Kalithia.

Nicola   No.

Alex   Why not?

Nicola   You know why not.

Alex   Tell me.

Nicola   Six weeks on a Greek island with a man twice my age? I may be C average but I'm not a complete idiot.

Alex   If I was trying to seduce you, why haven't I already attempted it?

Nicola   Scarcity of ouzo.

Alex   Plenty of red wine to hand.

Nicola   Not enough red wine in the entire Beaujolais region, sadly.

Alex   Alcopops?

Nicola   I'd die of diabetes before you got my top off.

Alex   I'm not trying to seduce you.

Nicola   Well, good.

Alex   But I think you should come.

Nicola   Well, I think not.

Alex   I think I could make you change your mind.

Nicola   No, you couldn't.

Alex   Yes, I could.

Nicola   How's that?

Alex   Read the label.

He hands her the canister. She reads the label with difficulty.

Nicola   'Uninvited . . . ?'

Alex   . . . 'Guest.'

Nicola   *The Uninvited Guest.* I've never heard of it.

Alex   Peel back the editor's log. There's another label underneath. Look at the signature.

Nicola   Jesus wept. Fuck. My passport's in Oldham. When are you flying?

Alex   Friday morning.

Nicola   I'll get it red-starred. I'll need some factor twenty, I burn really easily. I've no fucking shoes.

Alex   There's nothing sweeter than the enthusiasm of a sceptic.

Nicola   I can't pay my fare or anything, you realise that?

Alex   Not an issue.

Nicola   Are you sure this is genuine?

Alex   I think so.

Nicola   But I've never heard of it.

Alex   So?

Nicola   I've never even *heard* of it . . .

Alex   . . . and so?

Nicola   Jesus on the fucking half-shell, I've never even heard of it!

Alex   What intrigues me rather more . . . is neither have I.

Nicola   So why haven't you opened this?

Alex   I drove my mother mad refusing to open Christmas presents until about January the fifth. I've always preferred anticipation to the actual event.

Nicola   But you haven't even *looked*?

Alex   I've spent half my adult life alone in cinemas. I didn't want to see it by myself. The rest of this is waiting for us on Kalithia, where we shall spend a very pleasant summer uncovering and possibly restoring the most

important discovery in semiotic history since the lost
Eisenstein.

Nicola   Why me? I mean, thank you, but . . . well, I'm no
one. So why me?

Alex   Well, it's even better than I imagined it would be.

Nicola   What is?

Alex   The look on your face.

*The room transforms within the void, or the void closes and another
opens to reveal . . .*

Scene Two

1959. Behind some scenery, **Hitchcock** *sits on an unplumbed toilet,
removing the bones from a Dover sole, which sits before him on a silver
server. The* **Blonde** *stands in front of him in half-slip and bra.*

Hitch   There is nothing more satisfying than a grilled
Dover sole. No taste nor texture to challenge the bitter-
sweet meat of this holy scavenger. A foolish-looking
flounder, yet its raison d'être; somewhat divine. Observe. A
somewhat utilitarian skeleton gelatinously fused to an
alabaster muscle and the filigree of a primal nervous system,
all tuned to a singular purpose. To oscillate over the gently
shifting seabed, harvesting from the descended filth minute
morsels of the dead. No pun intended but probably
inevitable, its sole purpose; to transmute necrotic matter
into angelic flesh.

Blonde   Are they French fries?

Hitch   Sautéed potatoes. De-boning provides us with
something of a challenge. To hurry courts disaster. One's
appetite must not mar one's discipline.

Blonde   I was hoping you might clarify.

Hitch   One is required by elementary good taste to remove the entire skeleton in a single gesture. The ensuing satisfaction having proved itself the only palatable sauce for a fish of such distinction.

Blonde   I need to know what you intend.

Hitch   Voilà!

Blonde   What I should expect.

Hitch   Are you a natural blonde?

Blonde   Up to a point.

Hitch   Beyond which?

Blonde   No.

Hitch   And you require . . .

Blonde   Well . . .

Hitch   Clarification.

Blonde   That's right.

Hitch   Of intention.

Blonde   That's all.

Hitch   I pride myself that clarity is one of my stronger suites.

Blonde   Well, on the page it –

Hitch   In my humble opinion, the page is a mere receptacle from which the image refracts like port through a cut-glass decanter.

Blonde   Oh, it does.

Hitch   And glimmers with the familiar glint of genius, some would say.

Blonde   Oh, so would I.

Hitch   Then what are your concerns?

Blonde   I was lying on the bed. A man, your man, the . . .

Hitch   The cinematographer.

Blonde   The cinematographer. He squats at the end of the bed and tells me to move my knee two inches that way. He asks me if my ass, excuse me, is bigger than average. I tell him from where he's sitting anyone's ass would be the size of a house. He says, 'This is the angle.' I tell him I've got a small head. He tells me he can't see my head. Could I get a robe or something?

Hitch   On your shoulder.

Blonde   What?

Hitch   Might I enquire?

Blonde   This?

Hitch   The bruise.

Blonde   It's a bruise.

Hitch   Indeed.

Blonde   It's embarrassing.

Hitch   For whom?

Blonde   I'm not particularly embarrassed by the bruise. More the nature of the bruising.

Hitch   Please elaborate.

Blonde   I walked into my husband. I was off balance. I had only one shoe on. I had a shoe in my hand. I was on one heel. I hit the door. The corner of the um . . . the frame, the . . .

Hitch   The architrave.

Blonde   Is that so?

Hitch   Your husband bruised you.

Blonde   No. The thing.

Hitch   The architrave.

Blonde   I probably deserved it. I say things I shouldn't. I probably told him the truth or something. Is it cold in here?

Hitch   You require to know what is required of you.

Blonde   Yes.

Hitch   The sequence is complex. The shot-list self-explanatory.

Blonde   I see.

Hitch   We shall shoot Miss Leigh on Tuesday and the body double on Monday.

Blonde   Monday.

Hitch   There will be nine set-ups. The back, the left arm, the ribcage, the midriff, the shoulder blade, the left hand against the tiling, the right hand as it grabs the curtain. A top shot as the knees buckle. The thighs. The blood.

Blonde   Blood?

Hitch   You will not be required to supply the blood.

Blonde   And the character's what, she's . . . ?

Hitch   The character is naked.

Blonde   How naked?

Hitch   How naked is naked?

Blonde   Yes.

Hitch   How naked *is* naked?

Blonde   Well, if you're naked, it's pretty naked. It's nude.

Hitch   There is, of course, an alternative.

Blonde   Which would be?

Hitch   To decline the employment.

Blonde   But how do you intend . . . she's *naked*?

Hitch   Yes.

Blonde   Why?

Hitch   She's in the shower.

Blonde   Of course. But why?

Hitch   Vulnerability.

Blonde   I see.

Hitch   Thus . . . empathy.

Blonde   Uh-huh.

Pause.

This morning, the man . . .

Hitch   The cinematographer.

Blonde   He said her breasts, excuse me, are enormous.
He said he could light *me* 'til doomsday; when *she* walks on
set everything below waist height's in shadow.

Hitch   So?

Blonde   So why me?

Hitch   What was the truth?

Blonde   The truth?

Hitch   The truth you told your husband.

Blonde   I never said a word. So he made a wild guess.
Wouldn't you? If I hit you with a high-heeled shoe, wouldn't
you?

Hitch   Wouldn't I what?

Blonde   You'd figure something was wrong.

Hitch   Indubitably.

Blonde   It was my birthday. I thought if he buys me the
coat, he loves me. If he buys me more underwear, I guess
we still have a chance. He gives me a sugar cube with dice

spots on it. I steal ten dollars from his jacket and I buy
shoes. High heels. So this average size ass of mine is four
inches higher off the ground and whanging around like a cat
in a grocery bag and I get in late and he says, 'Where you
been?' And I guess I had a really good answer to that one.
I'm not sure I can do this. I'm not sure what you intend.

Hitch   I intend to create the illusion . . .

Blonde   The *illusion*.

Hitch   . . . that a woman . . .

Blonde   A woman.

Hitch   . . . who could be any woman . . .

Blonde   Any woman watching?

Hitch   . . . any *ordinary* woman . . .

Blonde   Any woman in the *audience*.

Hitch   . . . watching this . . .

Blonde   This . . .

Hitch   . . . entertainment.

Blonde   Entertainment?

Hitch   That she could be . . . that women *are* . . .

Blonde   Are what?

Hitch   . . . are stabbed. Occasionally.

Blonde   Are they?

Hitch   I believe so. And repeatedly.

Blonde   Repeatedly?

Hitch   Once is uncommon.

Blonde   Repeatedly stabbed?

Hitch   They tend to be. Whereas men . . . a single wound
to the shoulder, a blow to the sternum. But women, as a

rule, repeatedly. Women stab once. Men stab repeatedly. Which, my dear, *is a clue*.

Blonde   And we see this?

Hitch   We think we do.

Blonde   Well, do we or don't we?

Hitch   Yes and no.

Blonde   In essence?

Hitch   Yes we do.

Blonde   And she what, she . . .

Hitch   She dies.

Blonde   She dies.

Hitch   Of course.

Blonde   A horribly . . .

Hitch   Admittedly . . .

Blonde   Violent . . .

Hitch   Death.

Blonde   And you see this as . . . ?

Hitch   What?

Blonde   You show this as . . . ?

Hitch   As if it happened.

Blonde   But what do we see?

Hitch   The focus will be shallow. When the knife's in foreground, it's the knife that's sharp. On the high angle, her arms obscure her bosom. And mother's arm, naturally, obscures the area between the hips.

Blonde   I'm pleased to hear it.

Hitch   Naturally, yet . . . intermittently.

Blonde   By which you mean?

Hitch   Frequently enough to cut. As it were.

Blonde   I'm really sorry, but I don't think –

Hitch   You may rest assured we shall create the *impression* of nudity whilst never gratifying the audience with actual nudity as such.

Blonde   Oh. Well, good. That's what I was . . .

Hitch   However. Creating such an *impression* will entail by way of procedure a great deal of nudity.

Blonde   Oh.

Hitch   *Yours*, should you so wish to be employed. I am obliged to go for a great deal of cover and you will be obliged to relinquish all cover for the duration. Have I expressed myself with sufficient clarity?

Long pause.

Blonde   And she dies on page thirty-two?

Hitch   She does indeed.

Blonde   That's terrible.

Hitch   These things happen.

Blonde   Lots of things happen.

Hitch   No event in itself is surprising. But the *sequence* of events is always unpredictable. I should be grateful for a decision before we wrap this evening.

Blonde   Halfway through you want to lose your leading lady?

Hitch   She dies if you see it, she dies if you don't.

Blonde   I don't think we should.

Hitch   Ah, but *then* you'd wonder where she went.

The void opens up from 35mm to 70mm widescreen and transforms to . . .

Scene Three

1999. A spacious villa. White space. A patio and a pool. **Alex**, *crumpled from flight and airport, stands very still gazing ahead of him.* **Nicola**, *in sunshine-yellow skirt, stands behind him.*

Alex   Someone's built a fucking villa.

Nicola   So?

Alex   Bloody great pink thing.

Nicola   Wasn't it there before?

Alex   No it bloody wasn't.

Nicola   It's a fantastic colour.

Alex   It's pink.

Nicola   I like pink.

Alex   I want to gaze at olive groves, not fat English backsides broiling themselves.

Nicola   It's a nice pool.

Alex   It's bloody well overlooked. I had a view of the olive grove.

Nicola   There's more over there. Olives all over the place.

Alex   I should have bought both plots.

Nicola   It doesn't matter.

Alex   Sod it!

Nicola   We're not here for the view.

Alex   Why do the bloody English presume it's their God-given right to invade every square mile of splendour within three hours of Luton fucking airport?

Nicola   Because it's paradise.

Alex   Parasites.

Nicola   Gaze in the other direction.

Alex   Christ, there's another one. Foundations; look. Another two, possibly.

Nicola   Is she naked?

Alex   Where?

Nicola   There.

Alex   I couldn't care less. The view from here was exquisite.

Nicola   It'll be X-rated if she turns over.

Alex   Oh, bugger.

Nicola   Alex, nothing's perfect.

Alex   Well, this place was *meant* to be.

Nicola   It's heaven; there's bound to be other people.

Alex   That's a contradiction in terms.

Nicola   Is for you. Can I open the champagne?

Alex   It's for later.

Nicola   I'll pour mine first then; that'll make yours about thirty seconds later.

She opens champagne.

Alex   Oh. I blame the locals. This whole money-grubbing rural culture, slicing up their heritage for a few quid. Backhanders in lieu of proper consultation. I know what goes on.

Nicola   Don't get upset.

Alex   You'd be upset if you'd spent a quarter of a million and it turned into Ruislip.

Nicola   Don't go off on one. You once devoted an entire seminar to traffic zoning.

Alex   I've nowhere to park.

Nicola   Buy a permit.

Alex   No!

Nicola   Well then, get the bus.

They drink.

I'd love to end up in a place like this.

Alex   Well, now you have.

Nicola   I mean when I'm your age.

Alex   I thought an acre and a half that wasn't England might . . . stop the rot.

Nicola   What rot?

Alex   Putrid remains that used to be my mind.

Nicola   Could you translate by a couple of decades?

Alex   Indian food was the first casualty. The first passion to subside. That one could have eaten *enough* curry was a terrible realisation. Literally a mortal blow. Then alcohol; beer bloats you, vodka leaves you numb, wine tastes as dull and familiar as I imagine a wife might. Which leads us to sex of course. Masturbation increasingly less a poor substitute and rather more the preferred option.

Nicola   Why?

Alex   Because the consequences ever more negate the event. Chicken madras burns your bowel, and I mean clinically, literally burns it. You drink all evening for one fleeting moment of euphoria and the rest of the week's in the bin of oblivion. And making love increasingly requires the radio on the next morning.

Nicola   I'd advise you against such cynicism if it didn't suit you so much.

Alex   You wait. The first intimation you might have had enough *sex* and you finally understand what death is for.

Nicola   Can I have a swim?

Alex   The ultimate release . . .

Nicola   It's so *blue*.

Alex   . . . is release from *desire*.

Nicola   If it's all so tedious, do yourself in. I'll burn you on the beach.

Alex   It's all right for you.

Nicola   Oh, because I'm twenty? Because I'm thin? Because champagne makes me dance?

Alex   Does it?

Nicola   What are we waiting for?

Alex   Don't be so impatient.

Nicola   I've spent five hours in a damp, spidery cellar sorting though half a ton of Pathe newsreel and old silent comedies which we both knew would be a) enchanting and b) not funny, but we finally found what we came for. Seven reels of it. Now stop equivocating and let's open one.

Alex   No! Nicola!

She heads inside and opens a decrepit old Gladstone. Inside are six more film canisters, all in similar condition to the first.

Nicola   Eeny meeny miney . . .

Alex   There's a procedure to follow!

Nicola   Oh, get over yourself.

Alex   It's a science, not an egg hunt.

Nicola   Then teach me. Don't make me beg, just tell me what to do.

Alex   Couple of chairs. Copy the label on to the laptop.

Nicola   Oh, I do the boring bits. *Quel surprise.*

He reads a label. She slides a floppy into the laptop.

Alex   These are rushes, at a guess. Three or four days' worth.

Nicola   You said it was a film.

Alex   I said nothing of the sort.

Nicola   A lost masterpiece, you said.

Alex   Whatever it is, it's unfinished.

Nicola   Which is why I've never heard of it.

Alex   The point is if *you've* not heard of it that's probably because you skipped the seminar to score some Ecstasy.

Nicola   Ecstasy!?

Alex   Whereas if *I've* not heard of it there's a distinct possibility that no one else has.

Nicola   You are such a pompous arse.

Alex   You think so?

Nicola   Arsy arsy arse.

Alex   He shot *Psycho* in thirty days.

She copies the labels. He opens a flight case, custom made to carry restoration tools. One side of it becomes a light box.

Whatever you do, 007, don't touch that button.

Alex *picks up one of the canisters, and a scalpel.* **Nicola** *stops what she's doing. They both pause in anticipation. He offers both to* **Nicola**.

Alex   Try not to disturb the contents say more than you have to.

Nicola   Me?

Alex   Open it. Carefully. It's almost a century old.

She opens the can.

Nicola   Newsprint.

Alex   Wadding. Unimportant. Put it aside.

She puts the newspaper aside.

Nicola   Oh, fuck.

Alex   What is it?

Nicola   Dust.

Alex   Don't lift it up!

Nicola   Dust and cinder.

Alex   Cinder?

Nicola   Fuck all else.

Alex   Damn. Can't have completely desiccated, surely. Oh . . . blast.

Nicola   The phrase you're searching for is fuck it.

Alex   Fuck it!

Nicola   Calm down. Hand me another.

Alex *hands her the second canister and walks away, too nervous to look.* **Nicola** *opens it with great care.*

Nicola   Never taken Ecstasy in my life.

Alex   Cheers one up no end, apparently.

Nicola   It's for kids. If you were hoping for recreational drugs; sorry, you've missed that generation as well.

Alex   Be careful.

Nicola   I'm being careful.

Alex   Well?

Nicola   A gobbet.

Alex   A gobbet?

Nicola   A gobbet of celluloid.

Alex   Don't touch it.

He joins her and polaroids the canister.

Photograph everything in its original placement.

Nicola   Considering we got it here in a hired Polo Golf, it's probably forgotten much of its original placement.

Alex   Look carefully where the compacted trapezium dissolves into the dust. Not your fingers! Tweezers. Now . . .

He gives the trapezium a blast of canned air.

What would you call that?

Nicola   A snippet.

Alex   A snippet. Two and a half frames. Two complete, one fragmented. Give it to me. Bottle marked Perklone, pour some in the tray.

Another puff of air and he cleans up the snippet with a lush make-up brush. **Nicola** *prepares the Perklone. He uses a scalpel to separate the snippet from the gobbet and slides the former into the solution.*

The trick is to separate the layers, without letting the images tear or transpose or self-destruct.

Nicola   How much can we save?

Alex   At this rate I'd estimate around half a per cent.

Nicola   Is that all?

Alex   We should be able to reconstruct some kind of storyboard. Rephotograph the images. Any consecutive frames could be run on fresh stock.

Nicola   How likely is that?

Alex   Not very.

Nicola   Fuck it, Alex. What are we doing here?

Alex *concludes a deft bit of work with a Q-tip, and hangs the snippet up.*

Alex   Three frames. Two complete.

Nicola   Let me see.

Alex   Let it dry.

Nicola   I want to see.

Alex   Leave it. If the solvent gets under the emulsion, the image'll slide. Let it dry. Return to your trapezium. Use the scalpel. If there's a layer of celluloid that can be lifted, lift it. Do not cut it. Add a drop of rapeseed. Tease it. Persuade the dirt off.

Nicola   Push off, dirt.

Alex   Do not harm the patient. You only get one go at it.

Nicola   Then why are you trusting me?

Alex   I've no idea.

They work, slowly.

Nicola   Can I have more champagne?

Alex   You can have a cup of tea. In fact, you can make one.

Nicola   I'm busy.

Alex   I'd kill for some tea.

Nicola   How old are you?

Alex   I'm forty-six.

Nicola   Then I'm going to skip forty-six. I'm going forty-four, forty-five, fifty, sixty, seventy, eighty, good night and God bless.

Alex   You'll hang on by your fingernails like the rest of us. You'll take to your bed every birthday. You'll weep when you take down the Christmas lights. Your cousin who once showed you her bra will have a birthday party in High Wickham and she'll be *fifty*. And there'll be a disco and vol-au-vents. You'll bump into someone somewhere with less hair who says do you remember when we whatever and you'll say Christ that was twenty-five years ago and suddenly you'll realise *everything* was twenty-five years ago. Three times a day someone will ask you a question the answer to which is twenty-five years ago. You'll think about decorating and then you'll think, my God I'll miss this wallpaper, then you'll be awake until three remembering all the wallpaper you ever knew. Noddy. Tomatoes on kitchen scales. Flock roses. You'll walk out to the garden and you'll wonder how on earth that lilac grew so tall. Then you'll wonder how much taller it'll grow before it grows without you there to wonder.

Nicola   Well, well. What a coincidence.

Alex   What have you got?

Nicola   Flock roses, as it happens. And a face. Medium close-up. Foggy, but a face.

Alex   Let me see.

Nicola   I think I found the leading lady.

Alex   How do you know she's his leading lady?

Nicola   She's a blonde.

Lights fade as, projected on to and dissolving one of the walls of the villa, the grainy yet mesmeric image of a woman's face, slightly startled, an eyebrow raised. An immaculately posed, yet undeniably real moment in time.

Scene Four

The villa. Night. **Nicola** *has fallen asleep in an armchair, a Balthus dream.* **Alex** *is working. He stops to gaze at her. He swings an anglepoise towards her, or switches on a lamp close to her. Woken by the light she flies up and falls out of the armchair. A huge instinctive scream pushes all the air from her lungs.*

Nicola   No!

Alex   Jesus.

Nicola   What?

Alex   Sorry.

Nicola   What?

Alex   Just me. It's just me.

Nicola   Christ.

Alex   Sorry.

Nicola   Sorry. I was fast asleep.

Alex   Sorry.

Nicola   Sorry. What time is it?

Alex   Half past three.

Nicola   I was up at five.

Alex   Sorry.

Nicola   Fucking Gatwick.

Alex   I've um . . . I've finished the first reel.

Nicola   And?

Alex   Nine frames.

Nicola   Nine frames?

Alex   Well, nine intact.

Nicola   The entire reel? Nine frames? Has it dawned on you this could be a complete waste of time?

Alex   If you say so.

Nicola   I'm going to sleep until twelve then smother myself in Boots Own and lay on my arse for a week.

Alex   Your choice entirely.

Nicola   Is that a glint?

Alex   What?

Nicola   In your eye. Do I detect signs of life?

Alex   Tidy these notes away, will you?

Nicola   What have you found?

Alex   That we're spatially incompatible.

Nicola   Alex! What have you found?

She tidies, briefly, stuffing pages into a ring-binder.

Alex   Her fingers.

Nicola   Fingers?

Alex   Big close-up. I mean, really big. No one was using close-ups like this.

Nicola   Buñuel?

Alex   Years later. This is arguably the first. Third frame I looked at and already we've got a bit of cinematic history. Her fingers reaching out . . . camera's panned with her, presumably . . . reaching out towards . . . ?

Nicola   What?

Alex   Use the glass. It's slightly out of focus, but what is it?

Nicola   A light switch. She's switching on a light!

Alex   Here's another. I found it about a hundred feet on. Presumably the very next set-up.

Nicola   It's a light bulb! It's what I said. She switches on the light.

Alex   Don't jump to conclusions. There were two frames of the bulb on either side of this coagulated mass; measured across the reel, about an eighth of an inch apart. So we can estimate the length of the shot at about 250 frames.

Nicola   Ten seconds.

Alex   Give or take. That's from somewhere during the first second, this is somewhere during the tenth.

Nicola   They're identical.

Alex   Think about it. First few frames, last few frames.

Nicola   Single shot of a light bulb. Locked camera, possibly. Nothing changes.

Alex   Almost exactly ten seconds. Traditionally, when shooting a cutaway, the director expects the cameraman to count to ten.

Nicola   So, it's a cutaway! He wanted a cutaway of the light bulb as it . . . . as it *doesn't* go on??

Alex   It's off at the top of the shot, it's off at the end. She turns on the light bulb but it stays *off*.

Nicola   So, there's another shot.

Alex   Simpler. Think *story*.

Nicola   The bulb stays off.

Alex   She turns on the light . . .

Nicola   But the bulb stays off. The bulb doesn't work!

Alex   She's running her bath . . .

Nicola   Her bath?

Alex   Eight hundred feet on. Last set-up on the reel. This is the pick of the bunch. Reclining headshot cropped . . . by the edge of a bath. Blonde against enamel.

Nicola   She's beautiful.

Alex   Yes she is.

Nicola   Who is she?

Alex   No one I recognise.

Nicola   So she's running her bath. She flicks the light switch. Nothing happens. The bulb's out. So she's got to have a bath . . . in the dark.

Alex   Or even better . . .

Nicola   With the door open!

Alex   Backlighting her. A perfect silhouette. Blonde hair piled up, rim-lit, alluring. This little bit behind her ear loose, caressing the enamel.

Nicola   Cheeky sod.

Alex   It's 1919.

Nicola   And he's conspired to create the only lighting state in which he'd get away with filming a woman in a bath.

Alex   That's one interpretation. I think it's rather more to do with plot.

Nicola   What plot?

Alex   She's in a boarding house.

Nicola   How? How do you know that?

Alex   The door's open, so we can see the corridor beyond. There's a sign on the door.

Nicola   Something – oom.

Alex   'Bathroom.' And the one on the wall: 'Rooms One to Three.'

Nicola   Jesus, your eyesight.

Alex   It improves at my age. So you need more glasses. Glasses on your forehead, glasses in your pocket, glasses on the dash, all because your eyesight's getting better, which I think finally proves the non-existence of a rational God.

Nicola   You look better without them.

Alex   That's very encouraging. So. She's in a boarding house. She's in the bath.

Nicola   She's left the door open; that is so rude.

Alex   She's luxuriating. The corridor reaches out behind her. This creates a tension at odds with her relaxed demeanour. It's a typical juxtaposition. We can see the corridor more clearly than she can. Literally and metaphorically. She's in shadow, unaware. We can see the lit corridor beyond and are only too aware there must be some significance to this.

Nicola   Then what?

Alex   We don't know. That's all there is.

Nicola   Not much, is it?

Alex   Well, isn't it?

Nicola   Well, it's a bit audacious, I suppose.

Alex   But, don't you see what we've got?

Nicola   It's a scene in a bathroom.

Alex   Yes, but what *is* it?

Nicola   It's a nude scene. It's a naked woman in a bathroom which for 1919 is pretty . . . oh my God.

Alex   Indeed.

Nicola   It's the shower scene.

Alex   It's horizontal, for modesty's sake, but –

Nicola   It's the fucking shower scene!

Alex   It's *thirty* years before he finally used it in *Psycho*, but is, indeed, the shower scene.

Nicola   Do we know this? Have you got a shot of him, whoever, coming down the corridor?

Alex   No. But he's going to. Isn't he?

The images they've been discussing bleed on to the walls.

Scene Five

A small kitchen. The **Husband** *of the* **Blonde** *sits at a table, smoking. She stands behind him.*

Blonde   You wasn't here. I spent three days deciding. Round and round in my head. We need the dough, I don't want to do it. It might be good for my career, it might get around. It's 1959, my mother might see it. I feel flattered, I feel inhibited. I don't want to go naked, what, am I ashamed? . . . We *need* the *dough*. I paid the phone bill; we'll be reconnected. It was closed set. Which means there were only three dozen men hanging around. I was in a robe. Some guy brought me coffee. I'm shaking so much I splosh it on my hand. There's a guy and he's smoking and he's polishing a knife. So they point lights at me. I'm still in the robe. There's a lot of joking around. Everybody overpolite, like I was terminally ill or something. Then Mr H escorts me to the tub and holds my hand as I step in. There is some discussion in the corner; the props guy has his sleeve rolled up and his arm's being scrutinised and apparently, much to his delight, it passes muster. So they put him in a dress. Mr H stands beside the tub with his arms by his sides like a lifesize souvenir of himself and he says, 'Disrobe, my dear.' In front of everyone. Disrobe, my dear.

The **Husband** *takes a drag on his cigarette. She watches in silence. He breathes the smoke out of his nostrils.*

Blonde   . . . And everyone half turns away as if that's the
polite thing to do. And Mr Hitchcock turns his back. Even
the dresser looks elsewhere. I look around at how . . . large
this soundstage is, darkness looming all around and up
above. I'm lit like cut glass. The bow on the cord of my robe
has turned into a knot and it takes me time to undo it. And
I'm angry at the time it takes because I didn't hesitate but it
looks as if I'm hesitant. I'm being bold but I'm looking
nervous. Then it's undone. So now I have to open the robe.
So I do and I drop it off my shoulders and I hand it to the
dresser and I take a breath and all I'm aware of . . . is my
hands. i don't know where to put my hands. Not over my
breasts because that would be coy and that would give them
too much pleasure. I'd like to weave my fingers together and
casually hide my toots but my arms aren't naturally long
enough and to hide myself I'd have to stoop forwards which
would look ridiculous. All this thinking about hands happens
in the moment the robe leaves them so they fall to my sides,
so one reaches out and takes hold of the other, and they
hide, arbitrarily, the little curve of my belly. It's almost as if
I've never been naked before. So the dresser strides away
and as she does . . . every man in the studio looks at me.
Having looked away politely, now they look. In unison. It's
more than a glance, but not quite a gaze, cos suddenly
they're all extra-busy as if to say, 'I'm a pro, you're a pro,
let's get to work.' But in fact what I discern from this, what I
realise is, they can look at me all afternoon. That I can't
possibly look back at them all, so they will choose their
moments. I am theirs to look at.

The **Husband** *takes a drag on his cigarette. She watches in silence.
He breathes the smoke out of his nostrils.*

Blonde   So then it begins. A tingle in my feet flowing up
through my ankles and lapping my calves, submerging my
thighs. A warmth between my breasts flushing up across my
chest, rising through my throat, burning my cheeks.
Something akin to shame fuels this frisson, but there's no
shame in the feeling. There's pride in it and shamelessness

and excitement. A feeling of being there and nothing between me and them but somewhat more of me than usual. And gradually I feel better than I've felt for a long, long time. I glance upwards and there, high up on the gantry, is a man. No one but me knows he's there. His gaze is our secret. My heart begins to race. I think, Christ, don't let me get wet. But I'm tingling. I'm ringing like a bell, and no-one can hear me. And no one seems to notice. Then I came. I hardly moved a muscle. But I came. Can you believe that? You listening? I was afraid I would come, then I came. And you know the next thing I thought? I thought I wonder what'll happen when I tell him.

The **Husband** *takes another drag. The* **Blonde** *watches him. Then he puts out the cigarette, grinding it slowly into the ashtray. He leans back slightly and begins to undo his belt. The phone rings. He stops. She answers it.*

Blonde   Hello? Yes. Oh yes. Excuse me, but . . . is this really you?

Scene Six

Outside the villa. Dusk. **Nicola** *swims.* **Alex** *watches. He's been drinking.*

Nicola   You should swim.

Alex   I used to wonder why I didn't so eventually I did.

Nicola   And?

Alex   I almost drowned.

Nicola   You should *learn* to swim.

Alex   I don't like being out of my depth.

Nicola   It's fabulous.

Alex   Is it warm?

Nicola   No, it's cold.

Alex   I really can't see the attraction.

Nicola   Urgh. There's an enormous . . . what is it? Beetle or something, more like a cockroach. Big as my finger. It's got hairy leggy jaws at both ends; you can't tell which way it's pointing.

Alex   Survival technique.

Nicola   It can't get out but it isn't drowning. It's just wriggling along on the surface, oddly confident, sort of stoic.

Alex   It'll be dead by morning.

Nicola   It's the most revolting thing I've ever seen.

Alex   I hate insects. And I hate water.

An arc of water flies towards him, with the insect in it. He leaps up.

Jesus.

Nicola   Oops.

Alex   Gragh!

Nicola   Sorry.

Alex   Nicola!

Nicola   I'm sorry! I couldn't let it drown, I'm a Buddhist.

Alex   No you're not.

Nicola   I fucking am.

She gets out of the pool and sits on the side.

Nicola   I ask myself, am I a rising sun or am I a setting sun?

Alex   And which am I?

Nicola   You're a total eclipse. Viewed from Torquay in complete cloud cover. I'm smothered in bites.

Alex   Use repellent.

Nicola   What does it do, does it kill them?

Alex   I've no idea.

Nicola   It kills them. I won't use it. Is there *anything* you don't hate? Is there anything you might for instance – stop me if I'm being completely ridiculous here – anything you might *like*?

Alex *finishes his wine and pours another.*

Alex   *Vertigo.*

Nicola   Oh, if the cinema was built in the twenties but remains miraculously hygienic. If the print was fully restored, and the projectionist knows his aspect ratio from his elbow. And you're the only one in the auditorium, yes. I can imagine a smile on your face.

Alex   What was the first film you saw in the cinema?

Nicola   *The Care Bears Movie.*

Alex   I mean *adult* film. The first film you saw without your parents.

Nicola   *Mission Impossible.*

Alex   *Mission Impossible*?

Nicola   Yes. I was twelve.

Alex   Twelve?

Nicola   What did you expect, *Battleship Potemkin*?

Alex   Well, you're a media student. You must have been inspired somewhere along the way.

Nicola   Not really. Everything you tell us to watch again I've never seen in the first place. None of us have. We don't like to admit it. Don't like to upset you. Can this be my mini-thesis?

Alex   A thesis requires a theorem.

Nicola   I've got a title.

Alex   Not the same thing.

Nicola   'The Uninvited Guest: An Archaeology of the Imagination.'

Alex   I'll think about it.

Nicola   I wouldn't like to end up a mere footnote.

Alex   Would you have an affair with me?

A pause.

Nicola   What?

Alex   Would you?

Nicola   No.

Alex   I just wondered.

A longer pause. **Nicola** *wraps herself in a towel.*

I hope you didn't mind my asking.

Nicola   Fuck you.

Alex   I shan't mention it again.

Nicola   *In loco parentis*, you, you fucker.

Alex   Indeed.

Nicola   Indeed, in – fucking – deed.

Alex   There's no need to swear. I meant it . . . light-heartedly.

Nicola   You're nearly fifty.

Alex   I'm forty-six.

Nicola   And how many months?

Alex   Seventeen.

Nicola   That's nearly fifty.

Alex   Mid-forties, but I entirely take your point.

Nicola   I'm twenty years old.

Alex (*Mission Impossible*)   Pom pom pom-pom, pom pom pom-pom.

A pause. **Nicola** *gets dressed.*

It happens.

Nicola   In films it happens. Written, directed and financed by men in their late forties.

Alex   Because it happens.

Nicola   Of course it fucking doesn't. Unless she's an overweight retard from a council home.

Alex   I've been misled.

Nicola   Or he's Michael Douglas.

Alex   I think she makes him look younger.

Nicola   She makes him look rich.

Alex   Shall we just forget it?

Nicola   I'll tell you when it happens. It happens when an immature middle-aged man finds himself a repressed, damaged or parentally abused teenager and takes emotional advantage of her.

Alex   I see.

Nicola   Which may be an accurate description of you.

Alex   Yes.

Nicola   But hey.

Alex   No.

Nicola   So keep your sad filthy thoughts to yourself.

Alex   I will.

Nicola   Good.

Alex   In my defence . . .

Nicola   What?

Alex   Nothing.

Nicola   What?

Alex   An extenuating circumstance. Not important.

Nicola   You brought me out here to do a job. I trusted you. Please don't spoil it.

Alex   I'm not going to spoil it.

Nicola   Good.

Pause.

You have though, you've fucking spoilt it.

Alex   I suppose I remind you of your father?

Nicola   You remind me of my grandad. You'll excuse me if I don't go to bed with my grandad.

Alex   What was it about him?

Nicola   He played chess with me and Cluedo. He thought I could think.

Alex   Which indeed you can.

Nicola   Well, hey. Thanks.

Alex   Had I not believed you to be intelligent, articulate and relatively secure in your emotions, we wouldn't be having this conversation.

Nicola   If you knew anything about me, you'd run a mile.

Alex   You intrigue me. I adore you.

Nicola   This is a mid-life crisis, isn't it? I've been taken hostage.

Alex   I am acutely aware that what you choose to recognise as an alarming psychosexual aberration is as much a reflection of my fear of mortality as the divine cut of your skirt.

Nicola   Top Shop.

Alex   I am fully conscious of the sad and somewhat foolish autumnal state in which I'm kicking around, but I'm looking to unearth a spring crocus whilst you act as if some clenched phallic toadstool just thrust itself from the mouldering waste of my fifty disgusting years.

Nicola   Alex, I'm half your age.

Alex   An utterance no less clichéd than the proposition that preceded it. It should pull me up short but it urges me on. Less than half; so be it.

Nicola   Please don't lose the plot.

Alex   We both know the plot. The morbid yet somewhat endearing longing of a man on the slide. If I were a playwright this would be the play that virtually ended my career. If I were a novelist the BBC would pick up the rights for a post-watershed three-part series. If I were a photographer, my imaginings an exhibition, the council would step in and close the show. I am wholly mindful of the complete and utter unoriginality of this state of affairs, but here I am, and there you stand. And I adore you.

Nicola   You barely know me.

Alex   You are my faltering desire . . . made flesh. In defiance of my fears, all my regrets, you stand there, existing. Clueless of the power you hold. You stop my heart, you tie my tongue. I could describe every item in your sweet undergraduate wardrobe in words not dissimilar to those Proust might have used to describe eating a small pastry.

Nicola   You're going to wish you hadn't said all this.

Alex   I would surrender all the dull hours of my future for one moment's intimacy with you. Your eyes open, welcoming. Your thighs surrendering. To know all that's knowable of you in one ecstatic tumble would be to espouse all further knowledge, to find some temporary peace, some justification for continuing down this endless path of exhaustion I once recognised as a life.

Nicola   Does this ever work?

Alex   Never tried it before.

Nicola   Finished?

Alex   Yes.

Nicola   Nice attempt.

Alex   Thank you.

Nicola   I'm going to bed.

Alex   Well, at least acknowledge the cruelty of it! As the eyesight fails and my libido falters. The joke of it, the sheer irresistible insanity of it. Imagine me at your age, ignored by you. Imagine me in all the years between, ignored by an endless procession of you. Imagine. To have suffered all that unrequited love, then to have denied love, then forgotten love. To have finally outlived love and then . . . to love again. And for it to be requited. Imagine.

Nicola   You do remind me of my dad. He didn't have your vocabulary, but Christ he could bullshit. He used words on my mum like treacle syrup. Then she'd wait all night for him to come home with those words in her head setting hard, like tar.

Alex   I'm not your dad.

Nicola   You were eulogising about Ingrid Bergman being kissed in *Notorious*. And I was thinking, 'I really *like* him.' Next moment, I realised you were looking at me looking at you. You picked up on a little moment and it's become inflated in the memory of itself. I *like* you, Alex. But I don't fancy you and frankly never will.

Alex   I didn't expect you to fancy me.

Nicola   Then what did you expect?

Alex   I was rather hoping for an act of compassion.

Nicola   Well, I'm sorry.

Alex   Of course you are.

Nicola   I'm very fond of you.

Alex   Thank you.

Nicola   But forget it.

Alex   It's forgotten.

Nicola   Good.

Alex   Sweet dreams.

Nicola   Get therapy.

She leaves. **Alex** *drinks. Lights fade.*

Scene Seven

Terrace. Overlooking Beverly Hills. Night. A table laid for dinner. **Hitch** *sits eating Dover sole. The* **Blonde**, *dressed to kill, sits opposite, toying with rack of lamb.*

Blonde   So, Cecil B. de Mille died today.

Pause.

That Fidel Castro. He's got some nerve.

Pause.

Do you think the little monkeys will get back to earth?

Hitch *unpeels the skeleton of his sole.*

Blonde   Do you ever eat anything else?

Hitch   Why would I?

Blonde   For a change?

Hitch   Nothing improves on Dover sole. I have them flown in.

Blonde   Where from?

Hitch   Dover. How was the lamb?

Blonde   Oh, delicious.

Hitch   I was once sent an ear in the post.

Blonde   No kidding. What did you do?

Hitch   I buried it.

Blonde   I'm not . . . I'm sorry. I don't know how to act in a situation like this.

Hitch   You may act entirely normally.

Blonde   Well, this is how I normally act. This is how I act in a normal situation. But this is not a normal situation, so I guess I'm acting abnormally, which according to some is apparently how I normally act.

Hitch   Are you always this verbose?

Blonde   Oh yes. I'm bright. I have a natural intelligence that belies my background. So I have been told many times by men older, classier and less intelligent than I. So where's your wife this evening?

Hitch   Visiting her sister. Where's your husband?

Blonde   He wasn't invited. I borrowed his truck.

Hitch   The monstrosity in my drive.

Blonde   It's refrigerated. He delivers hamburgers. Not that he's a Neanderthal or anything. In the evenings he runs a restaurant.

Hitch   Indeed?

Blonde   Just another joint, but he hires and fires. Have you any idea the sort of *power* that lends a man? He's got a stick, he measures skirts. He divides the tip. He's gonna open his own place, blah blah blah, and these kids fall for it. I don't know, a tumble, nothing. . . I should care. Last three times we did it, it was the last rubber in the box. Excuse me.

Hitch   The one remaining rubber.

Blonde   He takes it out, he crumples the box, I think; hold on a minute. Did I forget five times? Was I *sleeping*? I'm sorry. I'm sure this ain't appropriate.

Hitch   You are no doubt thinking it might benefit your career if, at some juncture this evening, you were to place my member in your mouth.

Blonde   I beg your pardon?

Hitch   I believe it's traditional.

Blonde   I hadn't expected to.

Hitch   What did you expect?

Blonde   Thanks. A decent meal.

Hitch   I would like to reassure you that at no point will I require sexual services.

Blonde   Thank you.

Hitch   Dessert?

Blonde   I don't think so.

Hitch   I've unnerved you.

Blonde   Yes.

Hitch   Whereas had I sat here with my genitals exposed you would have known how to respond.

Blonde   Yes.

Hitch   You would have left.

Blonde   Yes, I would.

Hitch   Or you would have *knelt*. Or we might have developed a scenario whereby our intimate parts mutually displayed, we conversed about the weather.

Blonde   I do tend to feel the cold.

Hitch   By articulating the subject I have rendered you uncertain. You do not know if we are *discussing* this or if we are merely discussing it. I offer dessert and you fear acceptance may be construed as surrender when, in fact, acceptance will involve only baked custard and a spoon.

Blonde   And my mouth.

Hitch   Presumably.

Blonde   Or your lap.

Hitch   Indeed.

Blonde   I would like to be your next leading lady. I would like to be 'And Introducing As . . .'. I am sitting here knowing that what I say in the next ten seconds, what I do in the next half-hour, may transform my life to a dreamed-of place where I'm recognised endlessly while endlessly shopping, and the blessed respite of the blue of a pool and a calling for cocktails and the sort of pleasure that simply . . . sustains. Or I could go home again tonight and, well, I don't know. I could be beaten half to death. Or I could kill the man who beats me. Or I could run away and find compassion in some trailer park with a man who sees in me all the things he cannot have and we will learn the depths of despising one another. And he will die of stomach cancer and I shall grow fat drinking beer. Or. You could tell me I have a quality you can't quite explain and that no other could replicate and I am the one who must be gazed upon for you to tell your story. The eyes of the voyage, her eyes, must be my eyes. And I must be looked at and followed and murdered most probably but there will be a heaven on that opening night and I will ascend. And you expect me to know if I should eat a baked custard. You expect me to know if I would kneel or leave. How could I possibly know until you asked? Because, how would I know if there was anything between us akin to trust, or good faith. You put me, sir, in an impossible position.

Hitch   When I was a small boy I would occasionally eat a baked custard in the following manner.

He puts his mouth over the entire custard and sucks. The custard disappears.

(*His mouth full*.)   Delicious.

Blonde   I hope the little monkeys make it back.

Pause.

They didn't let Khrushchev into Disneyland. Apparently, boy, was he pissed.

Pause.

I remind you of someone?

Hitch   Why do you ask?

Blonde   The way you look at me. Earlier today you didn't look. You sat facing away in your canvas chair. All I could see was your name. You stubbed your finger on the storyboard, then the Jewish guy gestured and the camera came towards me and you walked away. Across the soundstage to the door in the corner which, without looking back, you stepped through and disappeared. Why didn't you look?

Hitch   Courtesy.

Blonde   You abandoned me.

Hitch   My presence was entirely unnecessary.

She leans forwards.

Blonde   Was it you? On the gantry?

Hitch   Would you like port with the Stilton?

Blonde   Did you masturbate?

Hitch   You have a very vivid imagination.

Blonde   I'm beginning to realise; yes I do. How far would you say a knife goes in?

Hitch   A knife?

Blonde   How far?

Hitch   Into what?

Blonde   A person.

Hitch   I've I offended you?

Blonde   I'm talking theoretically.

Hitch   Wounds to the chest?

Blonde   So far, or so far?

Hitch   It would depend on the angle of the blade.

Blonde   It would?

Hitch   A horizontal blade would penetrate much further than a vertical blade.

Blonde   Why?

Hitch   Rib separation.

Blonde   Oh.

He picks up the carving knife and demonstrates with her rack of lamb.

Hitch   Vertical.

Blonde   Vertical?

Hitch   Relative to the ribs.

Blonde   Oh, sure.

Hitch   Horizontal.

Blonde   Relative to the heart, lungs, whatever.

Hitch   Indeed.

Blonde   But in the shower . . .

Hitch   Mmm?

Blonde   The blade was vertical, the blood was inches deep.

Hitch   Artistic licence.

Blonde   Oh. That explains it.

Hitch   Vertical for the greatest effect, horizontal for the greatest efficacy.

Blonde   That makes sense.

Hitch   Why do you ask?

Blonde   Well, you never quite know, do you? (*She puts the knife in her bag.*)

Hitch   Are you aware of the recent innovations in the development of commercial film stock?

Blonde   I don't believe so.

Hitch   An improved richness of tone and hue, brighter chromatics, increased depths of field.

Blonde   I can imagine. What is it you want?

Hitch   There is a certain stock I wish to test. It promises rapid exposure but no loss of contrast. Brighter whites, deeper shadow, a greater intimacy with one's subject. If you would oblige me by performing a simple sequence, the resulting footage could also be considered your formal screen test.

Blonde   A simple sequence?

Hitch   A woman preparing to bathe, and unaware she's being observed, crosses to her dressing table and pulls back her hair.

Blonde   That's all?

Hitch   That's all.

Blonde   She doesn't speak?

Hitch   She doesn't speak.

Blonde   She isn't nude?

Hitch   That would be entirely up to you.

Blonde   How do you imagine her?

Hitch   Entirely nude.

Blonde   So if you did have a body to get rid of, how would you get rid of it?

Hitch   I'd throw it down a well.

Blonde   What if you didn't have a well?

Hitch   I'd reduce it.

Blonde   Reduce it?

Hitch   With a saw.

Blonde   That's what I supposed.

Hitch   Then reduce it further.

Blonde   Reduce it right down.

Hitch   In an acid bath.

Blonde   What's an acid bath?

Hitch   A bath full of acid. Slow but thorough. As long as your plumbing's up to it.

Blonde   Nothing less messy?

Hitch   It's a messy business.

Blonde   I'd hoped for something more . . . ingenious.

Hitch   Disposal is as crucial an event as the murder itself, for therein lies the risk of discovery. The car in the swamp remains buoyant. The pipes overflow and deposit something unpleasant in the downstairs apartment.

Blonde   So what's the secret?

Hitch   Don't dispose of it yourself. Force complicity on an otherwise innocent party. A lover is ideal. Spill some blood on their rug, get their prints on the weapon.

Blonde   They'd go to the police.

Hitch   To alert the police would be to risk incrimination. Even complicity is a criminal offence. Your chosen accomplice should have a degree of social profile, and a significant amount to lose. Publicity is one thing, bad publicity quite another. Damned if they do or damned if they don't, they will attempt to dispose of the body. If they succeed, the problem is solved. If they are caught in the act, they will protest but crucially . . . they are not you.

Blonde   You want to hear what happened to me, when I went home today?

Hitch   I must confess to very little interest in the mundanities of your life.

She rises. Undresses.

Blonde   I had a difficult day. I'll do anything you want.

Scene Eight

The villa. Morning. **Alex** *is working on the second reel when* **Nicola** *enters.*

Alex   You were up early.

Nicola   I went for a walk.

Alex   Just to wrap up the clichés once and for all –

Nicola   Is there any juice?

Alex   About last night.

Nicola   Ow. Ow, ow. Oh, ow . . .

Alex   What's wrong?

Nicola   Mosquito. On my ankle.

Alex   Well, brush it off.

Nicola   It'll fly off when it's finished. Go away! Oh, go away, go away!

Alex   Swat it.

Nicola   No! It's a living creature . . . ow! You little bugger.

Alex   I'd had a few drinks, I was jet-lagged, a bit maudlin.

Nicola   Didn't happen.

Alex   Good.

Nicola   Go away!

Alex   It's forgotten, then.

Nicola   I walked to the phone box. Called a cab to the airport. It'll be here in an hour. There, you see. Gone now.

She scratches.

Alex   I'd like you to stay.

Nicola   I am not the egotistic little nymphomaniac you hoped I was. I'm not like the rest of them.

Alex   The rest of whom?

Nicola   The girls he bamboozled and bribed. The ones he was seen with down the lane. The one he brought home. My mum was in the hospice. I found them on the sofa. She was a class below me at school.

Alex   I'm not your father.

Nicola   But don't you see?

Alex   It won't happen again.

Nicola   Good.

Alex   Even though, just for the record, I meant everything I said.

Nicola   Did you?

Alex   Yes.

He slaps a mosquito.

Sorry.

Nicola   I have to go home. You know I do.

Alex   I've examined the third reel.

Nicola   And?

Alex   It's distinguished itself from the others.

Nicola   In what way?

Alex   It's not entirely devoted to rushes. As far as I can tell there's a short edited sequence. Just a few frames, but all from the same foot or so of film. There's the first.

As they describe the shots, the images appear around them on the walls of the villa. There is a definite time lag, so that the images are only distinct once they have been described.

Nicola   Flowers of some sort. Lilies?

Alex   Soft focus. Her face beyond them.

Nicola   Her eyes are down. She's reading something.

Alex   That's the first frame; here's another, a few seconds later.

Nicola   It's identical.

Alex   Compare the lily to her downcast eye.

Nicola   She's lower. She's . . . what's she doing?

Alex   She's sliding down the wall.

Nicola   She's what?

Alex   Next set-up.

Nicola   A suitcase.

Alex   What's in it?

Nicola   Underwear.

Alex   White underwear, black underwear.

Nicola   The virgin, the whore, blah blah blah . . .

Alex   She's reaching inside. But what for?

Nicola   The stockings?

Alex   Every frame he chose pertained to plot. He wouldn't cut from one thing to another unless the cut had intrinsic meaning. So what's the story?

Nicola   She reads something we can't see, she slides down the wall. She opens her suitcase and takes out her stockings.

Alex   Which stockings?

Nicola   The black ones?

Alex   One more clue. Another two shots of the hall. She's walking towards the door. Spot the difference.

Nicola   No lilies.

Alex   Look closer.

Nicola   The vase is empty.

Alex   Because?

Nicola   They're in her hand.

Alex   Bad news, black silk stockings, a handful of lilies. Where's she going?

Nicola   To a funeral. Someone died.

Alex   Someone died. The question is . . . who?

Nicola   I have to go.

Alex   Stay.

She lowers her head.

Please.

Nicola   Alex, I've an apology to make.

Alex   What about?

Nicola   I was tidying up. I was putting my notes in a ring-binder.

Alex   Yes?

Nicola   They wouldn't go in.

Alex   Oh?

Nicola   Page without punch holes. A letter to you. Got mixed up somehow.

A pause. He takes the letter, puts it in the pocket of his robe.

Alex   Thank you.

Nicola   I didn't read it.

Alex   Good.

Nicola   One last swim.

Alex   Right.

She goes outside, comes inside again.

Nicola   I did read it.

Alex   Ah.

Nicola   I'm sorry.

Alex   I shouldn't have left it lying around.

Nicola   I'm not sorry I read it, I'm just . . . sorry.

Alex   Oh.

Nicola   I'm *so* sorry.

Alex   Thank you.

Nicola   It's a bit ironic.

Alex   Well, he was never averse to a little irony.

Nicola   Clinical fuckers. So . . . clinical. You think they'd .
. . . You wouldn't think they'd be so fucking clinical.

Alex   They're good people. I asked for clarity. A vague
diagnosis leaves room for hope. The consequence of clarity
is the loss of hope, which, for me at least, is a merciful thing.

Nicola   I wouldn't want to know.

Alex   Well then, they wouldn't tell you.

Nicola   What does metastasis mean?

Alex   No longer localised. The invading army has been
mobilised.

Nicola   Nothing's inevitable.

Alex   Well, some things are more inevitable than others.
Death in particular . . .

Nicola   Don't say that word.

Alex   . . . more a question of *when* than *if*.

Nicola   Look, I know a bit about this and you mustn't be
negative.

Alex   I haven't surrendered, but I've not a lot of fight left.
The whole experience has been . . . tiring to say the least.

Nicola   But no one *knows*.

Alex   One's body knows. The mind slips and slides around
it, oiled with hope one day and rigid with denial the next,
but eventually there's a *feeling* . . . not just the fucking pain
every morning, not that dull eruption in the joint, but a
fullness of feeling . . . you literally feel full of something . . .
unspeakable.

Nicola   It's what my mum had. She was afraid of it. She
ignored it, so I ignored it too. By the time we were strong
enough to face it, it was too late.

Alex   I'm sorry.

Nicola   You have to think positive.

Alex   I'm working. I'm in the sun. I'm with you.

Nicola   I'm going to teach you to chant.

Alex   No, you're not.

Nicola   I'm going to detox you.

Alex   I've been detoxed. I've meditated, I've been medicated, prescribed, proscribed and lethally irradiated. Then a staff nurse gave me a crystal, which is when I knew for certain I'd had it. You know, death . . .

Nicola   Don't say the word!

Alex   I live with the word. Not to do so would be a waste of time I haven't got. Which is as far up the path of enlightenment as I'm likely to get.

Nicola   I don't know what to say.

Alex   There's nothing *to* say.

Nicola   There must be lots, I just can't think of anything.

A taxi honks outside. They look at each other.

Alex   We could finish the reel, walk down to the bay, have a nice lunch.

Nicola   I can't eat anything with an advanced nervous system.

Alex   Would calamary be dumb enough for madam?

She goes outside. He drinks the dregs of some champagne.

She returns to the sound of the taxi driving off.

Nicola   Let's just get on with it. Remember the first shot we found: our leading lady?

Alex   She's dressed in black.

Nicola   So we've a blonde in mourning, and a dead man.

Alex   Bare bones of a plot. A film that was never completed. That only ever existed in his mind's eye. But we know his mind and we're very familiar with how he used that eye. Look at what we've got so far.

More images come up almost simultaneously. The **1919 Blonde** *sits at a dressing table, three reflections of her looking back at us in the hinged mirror. She leans hard against flock wallpaper, her hand pressed to her mouth. A cutaway of her high heels.*

Alex   All the usual ingredients, all the familiar themes; identity, trauma, moral irony, but what is it *about*? At a not-so-wild guess, I'd say desire. Terror and desire. Our heroine exists in mirrors and high heels and in the eyes of others. A man dies. I can't help feeling she's to blame.

Nicola   I can't help feeling she's in danger.

Alex   Guilt and jeopardy go hand in hand.

Nicola   If we're going to work this out we have to answer the crucial question.

Alex   Which is?

Nicola   Who is he?

Alex   The dead man?

Nicola   No. The Uninvited Guest.

Scene Nine

The kitchen. As before.

Blonde   Then I came. I hardly moved a muscle. But I came. Can you believe that? You listening? Like there was no choice; I had to come. And you know the next thing I thought? I thought I wonder what'll happen when I tell him.

The **Husband** *takes another drag. The* **Blonde** *watches him.*
Then he puts out the cigarette, grinding it slowly into the ashtray. He
leans back slightly and begins to undo his belt. Suddenly, the **Blonde**
stabs her husband in the back with a kitchen knife. He doesn't move,
but is very surprised. He gets up and turns round, his arms flailing and
failing to reach the knife. He staggers with intent towards the
Blonde*, who sidesteps him, comes around and pulls out the knife,*
with which she stabs him repeatedly in the chest. He falls over.

Blonde   So the First shouts, 'Turn over!', and the Jewish
guy, so quietly, says, 'Action.' Hah. This'll make you laugh.
The props guy with the knife raises it and as he does, he did
the most remarkable thing. He *looked away*. It's a real knife,
it's real close and he looks away. I couldn't help it, I stepped
backwards, out of focus, out of the light, I wrecked the shot.
'Cut!' shouts the First, 'What's the problem?' 'He looked
away.' 'I what?' 'You looked away. Do me a favour. Don't
look away.' So that was it. Permission granted. The naked
lady.

The **Husband** *crawls towards her. She hits him on the head with an*
electric iron. Pours herself coffee.

Blonde   Oh, the coffee break. Nowhere to put my cup.
Nowhere to sit without clambering out which meant
bending one leg and I don't think so. So I was in that tub
the entire afternoon. I was cold. And I was stiff. And by four
o'clock, not looked at. They had seen more than enough of
me by then, they'd had their fill. As we called a wrap, the
dresser was somewhere else and the robe was hanging on a
peg like thirty yards away, so I just hopped out of the tub
and ducked under a lamp and smiled at the gaffer who
smiled back and just stepped through coils of thick cable
and walked those thirty yards past standbys packing up and
the caterers wrapping the coffee; the nude lady heading for
her robe and something in me didn't care if I never got
there. Then I put on the robe and I felt like no one. I went
to the restaurant my husband manages and I found the
waitress he was screwing. I poured coffee on her. It wasn't
hot. He whacked me with the heel of his hand. Why he likes

doing that I've no idea. You'd think he'd break his wrist but no, he just liked using the heel of his hand. I went down. He kicked me in the hip. He threw me in a cab. He went back to help the waitress with her blouse. I drank a Jack Daniel's. I drank more Jack Daniel's. He came home.

The **Husband** *lifts his head. She seals his mouth and nose with duct tape. He convulses, then lies still. The phone rings, startling her.*

Blonde   Hello? Yes. Oh yes. Oh, we'd been disconnected. Temporarily. Excuse me, but . . . is this really you?

Scene Ten

The villa. Night. The pool is lit. **Alex** *drinking gin and tonic.* **Nicola** *appears from the driveway, somewhat dishevelled.*

Nicola   I'm a bit drunk.

Alex   There's juice in the fridge.

Nicola   I've lost my shoes.

Alex   Did you have a good time?

Nicola   They smashed all the plates. God, they must get through some plates.

Alex   Is that all you did?

Nicola   I had sex on the beach with six of the waiters, but I was too drunk to feel anything, so it doesn't count.

There's a shower beside the pool. She briefly sticks her head in it.

Sober now. They weren't real blondes, you know. He didn't want a *real* one. He wanted them all chemically treated. He had them developed.

Alex   Coffee?

Nicola   I hate fucking Hitchcock, fucking wanker.

Alex   Then why are you studying him?

Nicola   Because you told me to and I thought good, I'll just read your books and agree with you. Now I've watched the stuff and you know, some of it's really mediocre.

Alex   Mediocre?

Nicola   Unless you're obsessed.

Alex   Name me one film by Hitchcock that is mediocre.

Nicola   *Family Plot.*

Alex   Well . . .

Nicola   *Topaz.*

Alex   There's are moments in *Topaz* that –

Nicola   *The Man Who Knew Too Much.*

Alex   . . . is not his finest work.

Nicola   It's utter crap. It's got Ukrainian spies and Doris Day in it.

Alex   I think you should go to bed before you annoy me.

Nicola   *Psycho*: classic. *Vertigo*: classic. I'll give you that. *Marnie*: interesting, rapidly turning to offensive shite. *The Birds*: fucking weird. Everything else, patchy old rubbish. And don't argue, because it's a very thin line between worshipping Hitchcock and worshipping the 3.47 from Crewe.

Alex   There is absolutely no comparison.

Nicola   Frustrated sexual energy! Trains and films and small migrating birds. You're all wankers, the lot of you.

Alex   I may be. He wasn't.

Nicola   It fascinates me how fucking fascinated a man can be with a man who's equally fucking fascinated by ethereal blondes who aren't blondes in the first fucking place. And what sort of obsession is it that breeds the desire to throw

seagulls at them? And why are they all duplicitous whores?
And why do most of them end up dead? Sorry.

Alex What?

Nicola Can't believe I said that.

Alex Oh.

Nicola You've one foot in the grave and look; it's my
foot . . .

Alex I had to bunk off to see *Pyscho*. The girl in the ticket
booth was a girl from my school; she'd left the year before.
She knew how old I was, but she slid me the ticket. She'd
gone when I stumbled out into daylight, and I've never even
seen her since but I've seen that film, well, countless times.
And a few years later . . . *Vertigo*. A Technicolor symphony
to life and loss and longing. I was your age by then,
mesmerised by that depth of thought and colour, and
mesmerised ever since. One's journey from innocence to
experience is mapped by feverish imaginings and for me
that's for ever bound up with the images he chose to show
me that forbidden afternoon. He was the first man who
knew what the cinema would become. The place we go to
be shown those things . . . we should not be looking at.

Nicola Because we should not think them?

Alex Because we may not *have* them.

Nicola There are some things you need to know. Twelve
years old I was a bit fat. Thirteen I was mildly anorexic. I
have been arrested a total of six times. Twice for shoplifting,
once for soliciting (not guilty), three for drunk and
disorderly. I *have* taken Ecstasy. I've got some cocaine
somewhere, but I've lost it. I have been sectioned twice.
Once for my own good, once for everybody else's. None of
this is the sort of conduct I intend to repeat; however; it is
unlikely we could be friends for very long without my
stealing something extremely valuable. Or throwing it out of

a window, or being sick on it. No further information will be forthcoming. I just thought you should know.

Alex   I do know. It's in your file.

Nicola   Nineteen Eighty-fucking-Four.

Alex   You deserved a break. At best, the beginnings of a career. At the very least a good holiday.

Nicola   Your armour's a bit tarnished, Alex.

Alex   A little rusty with self-interest perhaps, but hey.

Nicola   Don't die on me. If that's what we're here for. If that's what you were intending.

Alex   I wasn't.

Nicola   Well, don't. I couldn't cope.

Alex   I'm flattered.

Nicola   I don't speak Greek.

Alex   Oh.

Nicola   You know what causes it?

Alex   What?

Nicola   What you've got.

Alex   No, I don't.

Nicola   I do.

Alex   Do you?

Nicola   Unhappiness. Misery. Not enough love. Is it late?

Alex   Yes, it is.

Nicola   I must go to bed.

She doesn't move. They sit there.

Oh. I know who he is.

Alex   Who?

Nicola   The Uninvited Guest.

Alex   How?

Nicola   Because I'm clever. She wears black silk. She's a heartbreaker. She broke his heart; she killed him.

Alex   Actually or metaphorically?

Nicola   It's Hitchcock; it doesn't matter. Which is a clue.

Alex   What?

Nicola   If someone kills you, *actually* you're dead. But if they kill you *metaphorically* . . .

Alex   You're confusing form with content.

Nicola   I'm not? The gaze of love denied is a murderous gaze. If someone breaks your heart, you want revenge. You'd like to kill, if you could only get away with it.

Alex   You can't take revenge if you're dead.

Nicola   Which makes it the best alibi you could possibly have.

Alex   Metaphorically.

Nicola   Or actually. He's dead. But he's not.

Alex*'s mouth opens as he comes to a realisation.*

Alex   You know something?

Nicola   What?

Alex   You're brilliant.

Nicola   Well, if you'd taken your eyes off me for a moment perhaps you'd have realised; yes I am.

Alex   Would I were born blind than to have seen but never touched you.

Nicola   I'm going to pick a fig.

She gets up and wanders off into the darkness.

Alex *reaches beside him and picks up the scalpel. He uses it to cut a lemon from the tree.* **Alex** *sits on the patio steps, cuts a slice of lemon, and puts it in his drink. Gently, the shower by the pool turns itself on. From beyond the shower, shimmering, naked,* **Nicola** *appears. Oblivious of* **Alex***, she showers.* **Alex** *stands and walks towards her. Coincidentally, he has the knife in his hand. He realises this, and puts it down. She turns to see him coming. Reaches out her arms. He steps into the shower and as he does, she dissolves, disappears. He stands in the shower, becoming sodden.* **Nicola** *appears, dressed as before, from the other direction.*

Nicola   Alex?

She turns off the shower. He stands there, dripping. She gets hold of a towel and dries his head. Leads him by the hand and sits him down. Walks away. Slips off her shoes. She walks towards him and doesn't stop. They tumble backwards and she kisses him, committed, passionate, intent.

Alex   I'm a little confused as to what happens next.

She starts to peel off her clothes.

Nicola   She thinks she's safe, but she's not. Because she thinks he's dead, but he's *not*. She steps into the tub. She lies down in the dark . . . are you listening?

Alex   Oh, yes.

Nearly naked, she clambers on top of him.

Nicola   And suddenly . . . there he is. The man who's supposed to be dead. Who is, in fact, the Uninvited Guest.

They make love as the lights fade.

Act Two

Scene Eleven

The villa. Sunset. **Alex** *and* **Nicola** *have been at work for two weeks. Short strips of film hang on a rail, there's a celluloid jigsaw on the light box.* **Nicola** *is relishing the last of the sun.* **Alex** *brings the magnifying glass and a single frame out to her.*

Alex I opened the final reel.

Nicola And?

Alex It's odd. The sprocket ratio's different. I've no idea why. You seem to have lost interest.

Nicola I'm tired of black and white. I just wanted some sun.

Alex It's gone down. Look. I almost didn't recognise her.

Nicola Well, it's the back of her head.

Alex Remind you of anything?

Nicola Remind me.

Alex Hair swept back into a swirl that's somewhat . . .

Nicola Vertiginous.

Alex The penny drops.

Nicola *Vertigo*!

Alex It drops over-cranked at fifty frames a second, but it drops. This isn't just a dry run for *Psycho*. It pre-augurs *Vertigo* as well. So why didn't he damn well finish it?

She puts on a robe and goes to the fridge.

Nicola He's in *Psycho*-mode so presumably she comes to a sticky end, probably without her clothes on. If he's in *Vertigo*-mode as well she probably turns out to deserve it. It was

1919 and he was shooting slasher porn and they stopped him. End of mystery. How are you feeling?

Alex   Fine. What's this?

Nicola   Carrot and beetroot.

Alex   How does it taste?

Nicola   Horrible. Drink it.

Alex   I don't want to.

Nicola   Come for a swim, then.

Alex   No, thanks.

Nicola   Just the shallow end.

Alex   No. What's nagging me is the ceiling.

Nicola   You realise there are still rooms we haven't done it in?

Alex   Something's wrong with the set-ups on the final reel. The incessant low angle of the lighting, the proximity of the lens to the foreground . . .

Nicola   I want you to drink champagne from me.

Alex   Then to confound it all; the most complete run of frames we've got and they make no sense. A low-angle pan across the landing; her high-buttoned shoes in foreground. The shot's incomplete, but before the film stops running the image in the last few frames blurs. And here's the odd thing: it blurs *in both directions*.

Nicola   Have you ever done it with an ice cube up your bottom?

Alex   Would you please concentrate!

Nicola   He dropped the bloody camera. Let's get a camera. Have you ever done it with a camera?

Alex   Nicola, there is supposedly more to a relationship than farcical amounts of sex.

Nicola   Fuck you.

Alex   I'm sorry.

Nicola   Well, fuck you anyway. And your ageing rock stars and your French New Wave and your wine and your fucking taramasalata.

Alex   We have differing points of reference.

Nicola   We've fuck all in common. Ow.

She slaps a mosquito.

Fuck.

Alex   Murderess.

Nicola (*to squashed mosquito*)   I am so sorry.

Alex   You'll come back as an earwig.

Nicola   Possibly a failed academic.

Alex   Thank you.

Nicola (*quietly, to squashed mosquito*)   Nothing ends.

Alex   You're not a Buddhist, Nicola.

Nicola   You know nothing. You have led me from the path to the forest, yet in your forest there are no paths.

Alex   What does that actually *mean*?

Nicola   The forest of sexual entanglement, the lost path of contentment . . .

Alex   Well, pause for a while in the Dingly Dell of real life and do some work.

Nicola   You are the man who put the sin in cynicism.

Alex   Just because such concepts appeal does not make you a Buddhist.

Nicola   That's not the point. The point is, am I what I say I am or am I what *you* say I am? You can't just enjoy the bits you approve of and reinvent the rest of me.

Alex   I have a theory about Eastern thought . . .

Nicola   Oh, you are such an arse.

Alex   A what?

Nicola   So supercilious. Talk to me.

Alex   I was.

Nicola   You never talk, you lecture. You take the high ground or you take the piss.

Alex   In what way?

Nicola   'In what way.' Everything you say to me falls into two categories. The 'I know something you don't' category and the 'You're a silly fool, so laugh at yourself' category. I'm sick of it. You belittle me incessantly then act all bewildered when I get pissed off.

Alex   Bewildered?

Nicola   You're doing it now. You're being bewildered.

Alex   When?

Nicola   When you said bewildered; you were doing your 'bewildered' thing.

Alex   Sorry; you've lost me. I don't know what I said.

Nicola   Wounded.

Alex   What?

Nicola   Bewildered.

Alex   Oh, grow up.

Nicola   Belittling.

Alex   Can we get back to this?

Nicola   Certainly. Via the usual reference to some obscure *homage* by Chablis . . .

Alex   Chabrol.

Nicola   Who's Chablis?

Alex   Chablis is a wine-making region in France. Chablis is wine.

Nicola   Oh. I'll bet that's what Ray Davies drinks when he meets up with Eric Clapton, is it?

Alex   It's *absurd* that you've never heard of any of these people.

Nicola   It isn't absurd when they died before my parents entered puberty.

Alex   They're not dead! None of these people are dead.

Nicola   You said John Lennon was shot.

Alex   John Lennon is dead. Elvis is dead. Jim Morrison is dead.

Nicola   Van Morrison almost.

Alex   Do all girls your age have an aversion to popular culture?

Nicola   If it's popular with dickheads like you, yes! Ow!

She slaps a mosquito.

Alex   Psychopath.

Nicola   You are such an anorak. I can see you, age fourteen, end of platform eleven, with your wind-up Super-Eight.

Slaps at another. Misses. Slaps at it again.

Alex   Jesus. That's why the sprocket ratios are different; he's not using a Bell and Howell. He's using a . . . Debris Seven or a Cinex.

She goes to the kitchen and gets a killer spray.

They were compact. Clockwork or battery-driven. Developed for shooting newsreel, not features.

She sprays herself.

Nicola   Little fuckers.

Alex   Don't you see? He's gone hand-held. It's not even 1920 and he's gone hand-held.

She sprays the entire room.

So why does he abandon it? Why doesn't he damn well finish what he started?

Nicola   It's been a week, Alex. I keep a diary. First night we did it three times. Over the weekend, once a night. Following week, every other night. Second weekend, a couple of blow jobs; thank you, Nicola, my pleasure, Alex. Third week, nothing. Bugger all.

Alex   Maybe he just lost interest.

Nicola   In the project or in her?

Alex   Well, she certainly never appears again. Not in anything I've ever seen.

Nicola   Well, obviously, if he didn't cast her, she ceased to exist entirely.

She rolls up a magazine and violently kills a few more mosquitoes.

Maybe he lost the fucking plot, Alex, just like you.

Alex   Lost the what?

Nicola   Because pardon me for disturbing the film but a few slivers of ancient celluloid are not the main feature any more. I am. I'm the one you're supposed to be obsessed with. I'm the one whose underwear you finally removed and that leaves you with certain responsibilities, one of which is to respond when I'm feeling horny which thanks to your invasion of said underwear and subsequent relative disinterest in it I am feeling most of the fucking time! Now are you going to shag me or not!!

She beats him with the magazine.

Alex   Nicola! It's not a question of losing the plot . . .

Nicola   What?

Alex   Because there *is* no plot!

Nicola   Do I bore you?

Alex   The image blurs in both directions.

He gets some snippets.

Nicola   If you need me, I'll be on the cutting-room floor.

Alex   What do you see in the top-right corner?

Nicola   Another bloody light bulb.

Alex   It's not a light bulb. It's a lamp. Ironically known in the trade as a Blonde. He's caught a light in shot.

Nicola   Is this relevant?

Alex   When a cameraman's unhappy with a shot he waggles the camera. He's annoyed with himself; so he spoils the shot. The image blurs in both directions.

Nicola   Why's this so important?

Alex   Because he caught the lamp in shot because the lamp's too low. The lamp is too low because it's rigged under the ceiling. So why is there a ceiling?

Nicola   Why wouldn't there be a fucking ceiling?

Alex   Because there wouldn't be. Not if they needed to rig a light there. Scenery moves. Ceilings fly out. But here we've got walls, doors, ceilings . . . and they're *fixed*. They're in the way. Which is why all the shots feel cramped and claustrophobic.

Nicola   So; he's not shooting in a studio; they're on location.

Alex   He barely went on location until *Shadow of a Doubt.*

Nicola   But he's shooting in a house.

Alex   He's using a small hand-held camera, and he's shooting in a house.

Nicola   So the seventh reel . . .

Alex   . . . is not *The Uninvited Guest.*

Nicola   Then what is it?

Alex   It's a home movie.

Scene Twelve

Villa poolside. Night. Played simultaneously with: inner sanctum. Antique cameras and film equipment. Pristine film canisters, displayed and lit like cut glass. Film lamps on stands.

*Inner sanctum. The **Blonde**, in black half-slip and bra, stands in the middle of the room. **Hitch** finishing his second dessert, a tiramisu.*

Hitch   Your clothing will drop into shot just here. You will walk to the dressing table there. You will sweep up your hair and clasp it behind you. The requisite modesty will be maintained by the sensitivity of the emulsion and the subtlety of the key light. Not to mention the angle of the lens.

Blonde   I wasn't going to.

Hitch *adjusts a light, rolls the camera and slates the shot. She caresses a projector that points at us, briefly mirroring its curves with her own. She peers closely at a single frame of the film that's threaded on the projector.*

Blonde   Flowers?

Hitch   Lilies.

Blonde   A young woman.

Hitch   Indeed.

Blonde   Is she famous?

Hitch   She was . . . promising.

Blonde   What happened to her?

Hitch   Please do not touch the equipment.

Blonde   She reminds me of someone.

Hitch *takes the camera from the tripod.*

Hitch   Are you ready?

Blonde   Are people going to see this?

Hitch   No.

Blonde   Then I'm ready.

Hitch *rolls the camera, then angles it at her feet.*

Hitch   And . . .

He *continues to shoot the* **Blonde**.

. . . action.

The **Blonde** *takes off her underwear and drops it into shot. As she crosses and sits,* **Hitch** *tilts up. As she puts up her hair, he dollies in, developing the shot to a close-up.*

Hitch   And cut. Your left foot.

Blonde   What about it?

Hitch   It wobbled.

The villa poolside.

Alex *sits by the pool.* **Nicola** *appears in her nightclothes.*

Nicola   Are you coming to bed?

Alex   He went hand-held. Take the camera off the mount and it moves like we do. It can see the way we see. Observe as she passes, move closer, caress . . .

Nicola   Alex, can I ask you a question?

Alex   *Psycho* was so successful, he planned a film called *Kaleidoscope*.

Nicola   Why am I here?

Alex   Early sixties. Psychodelia, sexual freedom . . .

Nicola   I know you wanted me, or frankly, you'd never have got me.

Alex   . . . killer on the loose.

Nicola   So here I am.

Alex   *Kaleidoscope* was never made.

Nicola   In every room . . .

Alex   *The Uninvited Guest* . . .

Nicola   . . . undressable.

Alex   . . . was never finished.

Nicola   So why don't you undress me any more?

Alex   The only thing that was ever shot were some camera tests. A woman disrobes, sits at an imaginary dresser, puts up her hair . . .

Nicola   It's in *Psycho*.

Alex   Virtually, but not quite.

Nicola *moves in front of* **Alex***, takes his hands and puts them beneath her T-shirt.*

Alex   The test shots are all that exist of *Kaleidoscope*; it was never begun. *The Uninvited Guest* was begun, but was never finished. The shoot lasts less than a week, then just stops. And somewhere in there he takes her home and films her.

Nicola   You used to stare at my breasts. I used to get embarrassed.

Alex   We're at the end of the reel.

Nicola   You put your tongue in me. Once.

Alex   And it's as if he's dreaming.

Nicola   Then another time. Then never again.

Alex   He films this girl, he lingers over her; you can almost feel the longing.

Nicola   Alex . . .

Alex   He saw Tippi Hedren in a commercial and auditioned her for three days.

Nicola   Alex.

Alex   She had to dye her hair. She had to pretend to be Grace Kelly.

Nicola   Alex, please! I know there's a problem and I need to know if it's me.

Alex   I should never have touched you.

Nicola *bounces away from* **Alex**.

The inner sanctum.

Hitch *and the* **Blonde** *are back in position.*

Hitch   And cut. You may dress.

Blonde   Are we finished?

Hitch   One aspires to express all that requires expression in a single developing shot.

Blonde   I see. OK.

She picks up her clothes.

Hitch   Modesty, please. You may get dressed in the hall.

Pause.

Blonde   You want to touch?

Hitch   The sequence is complete, thank you.

She moves in front of him. He doesn't meet her gaze.

Blonde   You can touch. I don't damage so easy.

Hitch   Nuance is eloquence. Intimation the ultimate intimacy. Whereas the overt expression of sexual . . .

She lifts his hand, touches her breast with his fingers.

. . . cut.

She clasps his hand fully around her breast. His knees buckle and he collapses.

Madam, we have wrapped for the evening.

He crawls to his chair and pulls himself into it.

The villa poolside.

Nicola *speaks to* **Alex** *from a distance.*

Nicola   I love you. I think. I think I do.

Alex   I don't want you to.

Nicola   That what happens to girls, I think.

Alex   I don't want you to love me.

Nicola   You take their underwear off them; and they do. I think. I really do. And this . . . what is this?

Alex   What?

Nicola   This feeling! What is this if it isn't?

Alex   Isn't?

Nicola   Love. Love is what? It's loving back or is it all alone? Is it feelings or the person? Which comes first; the person or the thing? The thing you felt. The thing. This thing. Why is this thing in me and you don't feel it anymore?

Alex   However cruel.

Nicola   Yes, cruel.

Alex   Nicola, this is my last fucking summer. I'm scared to death and I'm full of regret for all the things I'm never going to see or touch, so yes, I fell for you. But for all the same reasons; I cannot be with you. Your life stretches into an infinite number of possibilities the worst of which would be to spend the next year trying to pretend it wasn't my last. And the next few having to forget me.

Nicola   I'd never forget you . . .

Alex   I'm dying! Get that into your skull! I'm virtually a dead man! We'll get back home. We'll finish the work. We'll be friends.

Nicola   Friends?

Alex   I can imagine from your perspective that's not a word that means a lot. But believe me; eventually it knocks love into a cocked hat. Love you will discover, and this I swear is transient. Friendship endures.

Nicola   Does it?

Alex   Yes, it does. And I would consider it a blessing if you were to become my friend.

Nicola   Friend.

Alex   And we shouldn't underestimate what we've achieved here.

Nicola   You know what? Maybe he never intended to finish it. Maybe it was all . . . an audition.

Alex   An experiment perhaps.

Nicola   How to jerk off. Hand-held. I've wasted three weeks of my life attempting to restore a wet dream. Or two.

Alex   Friends then?

Nicola   Friends.

Alex   Can't you see what we've got here? This is huge.
This is a book. This is possibly a *South Bank Show*. A movie,
even. I'm giving you twenty per cent. At the very least it'll
pay off your loan. And the eighty quite possibly provide me
with a tidy little pension.

Nicola *hears what he just said*.

Nicola (*quietly*)   A what?

Alex   And don't think you're going to be languishing
somewhere down a list of acknowledgements. I thought a
dedication with a touch of mystery: To Janet Leigh, Kim
Novak, Tippi Hedren . . . and you.

Nicola   With what?

Alex   What?

Nicola   I once went out with a boy, I was seventeen, he
was deaf and dumb. He came up to me at a party with his
friend and his friend told me this boy really liked me and
they were doing sign language and lip-reading. And he was
cute, this boy, so I spoke really slowly and I did some
signing, sort of freestyle sign and his friend went off and we
sort of had a silent conversation. Then we danced and he
walked me home and anyway, my auntie was in
Scarborough so I went to bed with him. My first time. I
woke up in the morning and looked at him sleeping there
and it felt wonderful, even if he was a bit disabled. Then he
sat up and he kissed me and he said, 'Make us a cup of tea.'
So I made him a cup of tea, and asked if he took sugar and
he said yes. He wasn't deaf, or dumb.

Alex   I'm exhausted. Do you mind if I go up?

Nicola   I went out with him for a while. He never
mentioned the pretence, and you know what? Neither did I.
Then one day he didn't call. And he didn't call back. In the
end, he was silent.

Alex   I really need some sleep.

Nicola   Are you dying, Alex?

Alex   I thought we didn't use that word.

Nicola   Are you?

Alex   You know I am.

Nicola   I read a letter. I *found* a letter. In my file. Would I find it in your laptop, if I looked? Are you dying, Alex?

Alex   Quite possibly. Possibly not.

Nicola   Are you ill?

Alex   Well, a while ago . . .

Nicola   How long ago?

Alex   A year or so ago . . . I was quite ill, yes.

Nicola   With cancer?

Alex   They thought quite possibly . . .

Nicola   What was the diagnosis?

Alex   Oh, it was . . .

Nicola   What was it?

Alex   The symptoms were identical. I had a series of tests . . .

Nicola   But what did you have?

Alex   Internal haemorrhoids.

Nicola   Were they treated?

Alex   Yes.

Nicola   Successfully?

Alex   Yes. It was very unpleasant.

Nicola   But you're not dying, are you?

Alex   No.

Nicola   Were you ever?

Alex   In my defence, I rarely feel one hundred per cent. I'm really very tired. I'm going to take a shower.

He leaves her. She sits, catatonic but for the tears in her eyes.

The inner sanctum.

The **Blonde** *follows* **Hitch** *to his chair.*

Blonde   What's the worst that could happen?

Hitch   Please. Whatever contrary impression you may have formed, I remain . . . unaccustomed.

She lifts his hand again and brushes the back of his fingers down her belly . . .

Blonde   Imagine I'm imaginary.

He gently withdraws his hand. She undoes his fly and slides his hand into it.

Wait for me. I'll be right back.

The **Blonde** *returns, carrying the* **Husband** *wrapped in a bloody polythene shower curtain. She rolls him out on to the floor.* **Hitch** *stands and stumbles backwards, astonished.*

Blonde   So what do you do? You don't do it in the first place, but what if you did? What then? You got the guy coming in tomorrow morning to fix the air-con, so what do you do? Call the cops? Sure; they'll clean up the mess but then, guess what? They hang you. They electrocute. One thing leads to another.

She wipes her hands with a napkin and puts on her dress.

So I put him in the truck. I'm going to drive and keep driving, I'm going to dump him in the desert, what the hell do I know? I never been in a situation like this. I'd like to survive it. I surprise myself. I'd like to get away with it. What does that make me? Then the phone rings. They reconnected. Serendipity. Life will take care of you. My mother would say. So he's in the truck; you're on the phone. I put on the dress. I drive over. Welcome to my world.

Hitch *collapses back into his chair.*

Simultaneously, **Nicola** *hears the shower go on upstairs. She looks up. She picks up the scalpel and goes slowly up the stairs.*

Hitch *rises.*

Hitch   I'm inclined to presume this is a practical joke.

Blonde   I wish. Someone sent you an ear? Did it ruin your life? It was beyond hearing; you buried it. I need your help. I want kids. I want a machine that washes dishes. I want some guy with an ounce of kindness, drive me to the beach. I deserve a life, at least. I'm a novice; you got the expertise.

Hitch *prods the* **Husband** *with his toe.*

Blonde   It's a refrigerated truck. You turn the ignition, it refrigerates.

Hitch   I'd be obliged if we could bring this charade to a close.

Blonde   Have you any idea how hard it is to kill a man?

Hitch *kicks the* **Husband** *in the thigh.*

Hitch (*to the* **Husband**)   I am vastly entertained but not currently auditioning.

Blonde   He can't hear you. He's one big dead ear.

Hitch   I'm inclined to stick a pin in his leg.

Blonde   Please do.

Hitch   I shall.

Blonde   So OK, we're not lovers, but I got your prints on a knife. You got his blood between your floorboards.

Hitch   A dessert fork should suffice.

Hitch *picks up a dessert fork.*

Hitch *approaches the body.*

Blonde   My story; it's a dime a dozen, another dull
domestic. But *this* story, boy. It'd run for years. He pulled up
in his truck, he walks in, I'm on my knees. You got me bent
over the fruit plate. He goes berserk. You defend yourself.
It's so obvious it's ironic, but as a murderer, you're a hell of
a suspect. For the love of Christ, would you please help me?
Please.

Hitch   If you dislike the sound of screaming, cover your
ears.

Blonde   There isn't going to be any screaming.

Hitch *stabs the* **Husband** *in the calf with a dessert fork.*

Blonde   What did I tell you?

The **Husband** *sits up with a sharp exhalation of breath. The*
Blonde screams hysterically. The lights go out.

Scene Thirteen

The villa. Dawn. **Nicola** *huddled by the pool.*

Alex   It's five in the morning.

Nicola   I've pulled my flight forwards. I used your credit
card.

Alex   I see. Did you get any sleep?

Nicola   I finished the reel.

Alex   Oh. And?

Nicola   Moody interiors, empty rooms, a corridor . . .

Nicola   An *homage.*

Alex   To what?

Nicola   To the one he lost. I found one last frame intact. If what he shot at home was meant to be part of the film, it would never have made it to the final cut.

Alex   What do you mean?

Nicola   Look for yourself. It's a mirror shot. Look in the mirror.

Alex   Jesus.

Nicola   Personal appearance.

Alex   It's his cameo.

Nicola   No. It's accidental. Look deep in the mirror and you can see the camera. It's a Cinex automatic; you were right about that. But the shot's an accident. And I know what happened.

Alex   You've unravelled the plot?

Nicola   The plot's a McGuffin. What happened to *her*.

Alex   You can't possibly know what happened to her.

Nicola   She's in front of the mirror. He's behind her. The camera's electric. He was used to hand-cranking. He put the camera down . . .

Alex   . . . But he forgot to turn it off.

Nicola   So he's caught in the mirror, but he can't see the camera and he can't see himself. All he can see is her. All he can do is move closer. Look at the look. Look at the look on her face.

Alex   What happened?

Nicola   Look at her camisole. It's fallen loose. Look at the bottom-left of frame.

Alex   It's out of focus.

Nicola   It's his hand.

Alex   He touched her.

Nicola   He touched.

Alex   The look on her face.

Nicola   She'd taken a bath for this man, she'd sat in her scanties all morning and she'd frozen half to death. She trusted him, and he touched. Look at the look on her face.

Alex   Is there any more of this?

Nicola   Nothing. A few blurred frames. Whatever happened next between them, this was the last thing they shot. I think she left. I don't think she came back. It's her, Alex. It's the Blonde. He remade them all in her image. He pursued his desires and she punished him by disappearing.

Alex   *Vertigo*.

Nicola   She brought the promise of pleasure and the world went mad.

Alex   *The Birds*.

Nicola   She was beautiful and kind, but a whore he shouldn't touch.

Alex   *Psycho*. You don't think . . . ?

Nicola   He didn't kill her in the bathroom, Alex. He could murder one whenever he felt like it and they could still go home at night.

Alex   Lucky him.

Nicola   Lucky them. Do you have any Elastoplast?

Alex   What for?

Nicola   I couldn't find any.

She goes to the pool.

It wasn't me you wanted, was it? It was the *getting* of me.

Alex   Are you all right?

Nicola   Look at me, Alex. In the pool. Beyond all the ripples that distort me. I'm never still, I'm twenty-four glimpses per second. Look, Alex.

She lifts her top, or takes it off. She has cut the underside of each breast, a thin line of scarlet.

I've been a bit stupid. Not very deep. Just a bit daft.

Scene Fourteen

The inner sanctum. The **Husband** *has his shirt off and is covered in little crosses of Elastoplast. The* **Blonde** *tends to him.* **Hitch** *hovers.*

Blonde   So how much blood would a person have to lose to actually die?

Hitch   You made a number of errors. The angle of incision.

Blonde   Artistic licence.

Hitch   Indeed.

The **Husband**'s *head falls forwards.*

Blonde   Don't drop off, honey. Stay awake. I hit him with the iron.

Hitch   Not hard enough.

Blonde   Six times. There was blood coming out of his ear.

Hitch   Perforated eardrum.

Blonde   I sealed his mouth and nose with duct tape.

Hitch   He breathed through his ear.

Blonde   You can breath through your ear?

Hitch   Only if someone has the foresight to perforate your eardrum.

The **Husband***'s head falls forwards.*

Blonde Honey?

Hitch It would be infinitely preferable if he maintained consciousness.

Blonde I froze him in the back of a meat truck.

Hitch Your most significant error of all. The likelihood of bleeding to death being inversely proportionate to the rate of circulation.

Blonde I don't think he can hear us. I think he's going to die again.

Hitch It's imperative that he does not.

Blonde I don't think he knows that

Hitch Attract his attention.

Blonde He never paid me any.

His head flops.

Honey, keep your head up or the blood comes out your ear.

Hitch Might I suggest cold water and a loud noise?

Blonde They sank his ship at Pearl Harbor. He slept through it. You show movies in here?

Hitch I screen the occasional picture.

Blonde Show him a movie.

Hitch A movie?

Blonde He'd never die in the middle of a movie. It's the only time he's ever fully conscious. Whatever's on the thing.

Hitch . . . Is entirely unsuitable.

Blonde If it's a picture and it moves, he'll be alive until the credits. How do you work this thing?

Hitch Please, desist.

Blonde   Trust me.

Hitch   Nothing on this reel was intended for public consumption.

The **Husband** *almost falls from the chair.*

Blonde   Oh Jesus. Will you turn that damn thing on?

Hitch   The footage is purely personal.

Blonde   You any idea what they do to fat men in the penitentiary?

Hitch *turns on the projector. The screens come alive with the lost footage, in rough-cut.*

Blonde   Look at the screen, honey, look at the pictures. Look at the pretty lady. Do you have any popcorn?

Hitch *is entranced by the images. She joins him.*

Blonde   Who was she?

Hitch   She was . . . promising. Note how she remains perfectly still as she disrobes.

Blonde   You know who she reminds me of? Honey? You think she looks like me? This seems familiar.

Hitch   I think you should keep your eye . . . on our uninvited guest.

Blonde   My, weren't they modest in those days.

Hitch   You are privy to my ultimate confession. I was only ever . . . a voyeur.

The **1919 Blonde** *at a dressing table.* **Hitch** *appears, caught in a mirror shot.*

Blonde   Well, hi there, little man.

Hitch   Beyond which we need not venture.

He moves to the projector.

Blonde   Don't touch that. Don't touch!

Hitch's *hand reaching into frame, touching the* **1919 Blonde**.

Blonde   Well, what do you know?

Hitch *slips down the straps of the* **Blonde**'s *chemise.*

The **Husband** *falls off his chair.*

Blonde   Don't you die! Don't you dare die!

She gives him a flying kick. He groans, struggles to his feet. The **1919 Blonde** *leaps up, jolts the camera, blurs the image.*

I love you, babe, I love you.

She grabs him and throws him against the wall.

Don't you die on me, you son of a bitch!

She swings the projector around. The light blasts his face. They are surrounded with images, all the sequences unearthed. The scenery goes wild to the whirring of the projector. He scrabbles at the light. A gurgling scream.

Love you, hon.

Husband   HAVE YOU ANY IDEA HOW MUCH THIS HURTS? HAVE YOU ANY IDEA WHAT YOU DO, WHAT YOU'VE DONE, WHAT YOU DID TO ME, YOU CUNT!?

The images slow down, caressing the **1919 Blonde**.

Hitch   Have you any idea?

The film runs out of the projector.

Husband   Have you any idea, any of you, what you do to me?

Blonde   I'm working on it.

Husband   Could we . . . ? Could we go home now?

Blonde   Sure.

Husband   Ow.

The **Husband** *leaves.*

Hitch *takes the reel from the projector.*

Blonde   So, um . . . do I get to be your leading lady?

Hitch   I regret to inform you, no, you do not.

Blonde   You touched *her*. Why not me?

Hitch   As this evening has demonstrated, to touch is to court disaster.

Blonde   Violence?

Hitch   Intimacy.

Blonde   I really need that job.

Hitch *is silent.*

Blonde   OK. Thanks for the dinner and the er . . .

Hitch   Elastoplast.

Blonde   It's a good product. I'm gonna get some. I'm gonna stock up.

She begins to cry. The horror of the day and the fear of tomorrow. **Hitch** *just watches.*

You know he's gonna kill me. When he recovers. Sooner or later. I'm dead.

Hitch   I'm sure you're being overmelodramatic. Good night.

Hitch *puts the reel into a silver canister.*

Blonde   Keep her right there on the spool, huh? Bring her to life any moment you like. If you liked her so much, what happened to her?

Hitch *holds the canister to his chest.*

Blonde   Is it true? In the movie? There's a shot down a toilet?

Hitch Yes.

Blonde They're gonna hate it.

She leaves. **Hitch** *sits, clutching the reel.*

Scene Fifteen

The villa. **Nicola** *sitting on her luggage. Sunglasses.* **Alex**, *sheepish, is packing the canisters.*

Nicola You never intended to touch me again, did you, Alex? Because touching makes us real, doesn't it? Touching me wakes you from the dream of someone else you'd rather touch.

Alex There was no need.

Nicola Recognised form of treatment for things that can't be cured.

Alex If you meant to shame me, there was really no need. I was ashamed enough already. I was ashamed before it began. If I was unfamiliar with shame, wouldn't be the man who did this to you.

Nicola Not meant to make you guilty, Alex. Meant to make me better. I've lots of little scars. I thought you'd notice them. Your fingers brushed them. I thought you'd ask.

Alex My only defence is surely true of all of us; we only ever take what we sorely need.

Nicola Is that the first one we opened?

Alex Yes.

Nicola It wasn't entirely disintegrated celluloid.

Alex Yes, it was.

Nicola Discard nothing, you said, so I didn't.

She produces a half-page of folded newspaper.

I kept the wadding. I thought it might help us with dates.
Three cuttings. *The Arts Insider*, November third. 'The life of
a young woman came to a self-determined end on Sunday
evening. Miss Alicia Arnold, who was reputedly discovered
by Mr Hitchcock whilst serving him tea in Lyons Corner
House, but scurrilously rumoured in certain pages not to
have been serving tea, but requesting the price of one, was
to have appeared in Mr Hitchcock's inexplicably cancelled
production, *The Uninvited Guest*.'

She hands it to **Alex**. *He continues reading.*

Alex   'One is tempted to conjecture that the promised rise
from obscurity to stardom, cruelly arrested, brought to a
premature end not only a promising career . . . but also . . .
a young life.'

Nicola   *Kilburn Chronicle*. November tenth. A photograph.
A funeral. Of someone so obscure? Of course. Because he's
there. No relatives being in attendance, Mr Hitchcock
received the remains. *Evening News*. December eight 'Mr
Alfred Hitchcock has announced he will be leaving these
shores for the United States of America. We wish him bon
voyage.'

Alex *fingers the dust in the can.*

Alex   All that's left of her: paper and celluloid.

Nicola   His sense of irony was always macabre. And it
isn't celluloid.

Alex   Well then, what is it?

Nicola   I think it's her.

She looks at him. He realises. He wipes his fingers.

Nicola   A lifetime of being looked at instead of loved.
Sometimes, Alex, that cuts *really* deep. I'm out of here.

Alex   You can't go like that.

Nicola   I'm gone.

Alex   I could take you to a hospital; we're fully insured.

Nicola   Fuck off Alex, I'm not going to a hospital. I'm going to Ibiza.

Alex   I don't believe you.

Nicola   I don't care.

She picks up her rucksack. Winces.

Ow.

Alex   Don't go.

Nicola   Go and have a lie-down; you look exhausted.

Alex   I don't think I could make it up the stairs.

Nicola   Maybe your mother will meet you at the top. See you down the Odeon.

She goes to the door. Turns back.

I'm so stupid. I know who she was. She sold you a cinema seat. You'd had erotic dreams about her all through the fourth form, and suddenly there she was in the real world, in the foyer. You asked her what time she finished or would she like a coffee or was she busy on Sunday. She just stared at you, standing there with your heart in your mouth. She slid the ticket towards you. You watched Janet Leigh. She died in the shower. You came out into the sun and she was gone.

She leaves.

Scene Sixteen

*The kitchen. Exactly as before. The **Husband** of the **Blonde** sits at a table, smoking. The **Blonde** holds the phone. She puts it down and stands behind him.*

Blonde   Maybe I never should have mentioned it. You'd never have recognised me. The way I look at it, you never know what's best to do but it's best you did it. You lay on your deathbed, you look back. You're the sum of what you got, not what you wanted. You get the kind of love you ask for.

She takes the cigarette from his mouth, taps the ash off, returns it to his mouth.

I see this as a great opportunity for both of us. A new beginning. I'm going to take care of you. I hope you see it the way I see it, because I remember when we met life suddenly made sense. I should never have bought those shoes. I'm making you chicken soup. It's out of a can but I'm adding chicken. We'll look back on this and we'll just laugh it off. None of us get what we deserve. Unless we deserve it. I know what I deserve.

She takes the cigarette from his mouth, taps the ash off, returns it to his mouth.

Remember the first time we went to a movie? When James Stewart takes her to see those big trees that go on and on in spite of them? And she jumps in the river and she falls from the tower but still she goes on. She comes back to him over and over, even though it wasn't her, even though it was. I liked that movie. You didn't understand it. You thought he was twisted. I thought he was faithful and true. We should go to more movies. Don't you think?

He takes the cigarette out of his own mouth. She turns and watches. A sound not unlike the ring of a telephone, quiet at first but rising to an ear-splitting screech as he grinds out the cigarette and she waits, tense with anticipation. He leans back and takes off his belt. He stands and looks at her. She grabs a knife and stabs herself, once, between the shoulder and the breast. Pulls it out and throws it in the sink. He walks towards her. She quakes, her feet frozen to the spot. He embraces her. She collapses, with relief, into the circle of his arms.

Scene Seventeen

Alex *sits at night by the pool. He holds the canister containing all the snippets, all the single frames.* **Hitch** *appears and sits beside him.*

Alex   A purely academic question. *The Uninvited Guest* . . .

Hitch   . . . was never finished.

Alex   . . . But had it been so, how was it to end?

Hitch   The heroine, beyond all expectation, lives to tell the tale.

Nicola *appears, elsewhere.*

Nicola   I left the course. I'd had enough semiotics. Moved to sociology. I only ever saw Alex from a distance. The closest I came was a few years later, on graduation day. I saw him, he didn't see me. And it wasn't in the Great Hall, it was in a pub in Selly Oak. He was in a corner with one of his students. I wasn't surprised. She was a blonde. And she had that look; slightly unsure, slightly blank behind the eye. Presumably he took one look at her application photo and offered her a place pending two Ds and a C. He looked happy. Like a kid in a matinée queue. For all the time I'd spent hating the sad fucker, there were some moments when he'd looked at me, and wanted so much to want what he saw, that all I could think of to do, was to leave the pub and leave him to it. And as I did . . .

Hitch *takes the canister from* **Alex**.

Alex   Of course, no narrative is complete until the protagonist emerges . . . a changed man.

Hitch   While on the contrary, mine are fortunate if they merely . . . survive.

Nicola   . . . I found myself hoping, beyond all hope of it being so, that he had found her.

By the same author

Terry Johnson Plays: 1
(Insignificance; Unsuitable for Adults; Cries from the
Mammal house)

Terry Johnson Plays: 2
(Imagine Drowning; Hysteria; Dead Funny)